Fundamentals of Python Programming Using Colab

Dr.N. Valliammal

Dr.R. Vijayabhanu

Published by

Fundamentals of Python Programming Using Colab

Copyright © 2021 by Bonfring

9 789392 537011 >

ISBN 978-93-92537-01-1

Authors

Dr.N. Valliammal

Dr.R. Vijayabhanu

Bonfring

309, 5th Street Extension, Gandhipuram,

Coimbatore-641 012,

Tamil Nadu, India.

E-mail: info@bonfring.org

Website: www.bonfring.org

Foreword

This book 'Fundamentals of Python Programming Using Colab' is intended for the students of Undergraduate level who can use the high-level programming language as an effective platform that runs in the browser using Google Cloud.

Python is a dynamic, high level, free open source and interpreted programming language often used to build websites and software, automate tasks, and conduct data analysis. Python is a general purpose language, meaning it can be used to create a variety of different programs and isn't specialized for any specific problems. Python is applicable for any stream and it is not restricted only to Computer Science. It plays dominant role in these days as advanced technology. It can be used as a scripting language or can be compiled to byte-code for building large applications. It provides very high-level dynamic data types and supports dynamic type checking. It can also be easily integrated with C, C++, COM, ActiveX, CORBA, and Java.

Google Colab is a product of Google and is basically a free notebook environment that runs fully in the cloud. Google Co-Laboratory is a Google cloud-based service and you don't have to install anything on your system to use it. This platform is very user friendly and effectively supports users to edit documents in a very easy mode similar to Google Docs. Colab supports many popular and high-level machine learning libraries which can be easily loaded in your notebook. Over many years, Google developed AI framework called Tensor Flow and a development tool called Co laboratory. Today Tensor Flow is open-sourced and Google made Co laboratory free for public use. Another attractive feature that Google offers to the developers is the use of GPU. Colab supports GPU and it is totally free. The reasons for making it free for public could be to make its software a standard in the academics for teaching machine learning and data science. The platform is highly supportive to write and execute code in Python with the creation of new notebooks.

This book aims to develop an environment that runs in the browser using Google Cloud. Google Co laboratory is primarily used by the readers that support to execute the code similar to a standard desktop setup to work. Each chapter of this book makes the readers walk through to learn and develop code in a very simplified way to analyze and visualize data.

Dr. Anand Paul

Lab Founder & Director, Connected Computing & Media Processing Laboratory

Professor, The School of Computer Science and Engineering

Kyungpook National University

South Korea, Daegu.

Foreword

This book 'Fundamentals of Python Programming Using Colab' describes and gives a complete guidance about the basics of Python Programming using Google Colab with examples. Each chapter in this book makes readers expertise the fundamentals of python. Python provides a balance between the practical and the conceptual framework and beginners can pick up the language and start immediately to work with problems of compilation and linking.

Furthermore, Python comes with a large library of modules that can be used to do all sort of tasks ranging from web-programming to graphics. Having such a practical focus is a great way to engage students and it allows them to complete significant projects. However, Python can also serve as an excellent foundation to solve real world problems which uses variety of features from programming languages such as C++, Java, Modula-3 and Scheme. Python's most remarkable features are its broad appeal to professional software developers, scientists, researchers, artists, and educators.

Colaboratory, or "Colab" for short, allows you to write and execute Python in the browser, with Zero configuration required and free access to GPUs and is easily sharable. Google Colab is an interactive environment called a Colab notebook that lets you write and execute code. Colab notebook supports to combine executable code and rich text in a single document, along with images, HTML, LaTeX and more. Users own notebook using Colab are stored in your Google Drive account. Users can easily share your Colab notebooks with co-workers, allowing the users to comment on your notebooks and even edit them. Using Colab it is very simple to access Python libraries to analyze and visualize data. The code cell below uses Numpy to generate some random data, and uses matplotlib to visualize it.

This book will be highly supportive for under graduate students and makes the readers walk through the fundamentals of Python Programming using Colab with simple coding and examples.

Dr. Vasantha Kalyani David

Professor & Head

Department of Computer Science

Avinashilingam Institute for Home Science and Higher Education for Women,

Coimbatore.

Preface

Python is a programming language which is easy to read and has a vast library of modules focused on solving the problems. There are many reasons to learn Python. It is a dynamic language in general and run across a Python code on the web. Python reflects a number of growing trends in software development leading to the edge of good programming skills. It is a very simple language surrounded by a vast library of add-on modules. It is an open source project, supported by many individuals. It is an object-oriented language, binding data and processing into class definitions. It is a platform-independent, scripted language, with complete access to operating system API's. It supports integration of complex solutions from pre-built components. It is a dynamic language, which avoids many of the complexities and overheads of compiled languages.

This book is a complete presentation towards Fundamentals of Python Programming using CoLab. It is oriented toward learning, which involves accumulating many closely intertwined concepts. The contents of the book with subset of statements and worked out examples guides the readers for easier understanding and provides guidance to work with a number of exercises which helps to internalize each language concept. While many books cover the syntax and semantics of Python, in this book we'll also cover the pragmatic considerations. Our core objective is to build enough language skills with more exercises to encourage further exploration of each layer and examples that help students master the concepts presented in the chapter. This book assumes a basic level of skill with any of the commonly-available computer systems.

Python is widely used in many areas because of its salient features. It is easy to code, and mainly it is free and open source. It is high level language and portable language. It has a very simple syntax that allows the users to write programs with minimum number of lines than other languages. It runs on interpreter system so that it can execute as soon as code written. The objectives of learning python are to get master in the fundamentals of writing Python, learning core python scripting elements, discover how to work with list and sequence data, make the cost robust by handling errors and exceptions properly, explore python's object-oriented features.

Google Colab is a product of Google and is basically a free notebook environment that runs fully in the cloud. The significant feature supports the users to edit and supports many popular and high-level machine learning libraries which can be easily loaded in the notebook. Google Colab is popular because of the support of GPU and that is also totally free. Google colaboraty make the software a standard in the academics for teaching machine learning libraries which can be easily loaded in your notebook and for the domain of data science.

Colab is also a long term perspective of building a customer base for Google Cloud APIs. Colab supports many popular machine learning. The significant features of Google Colab supports to easily write and execute code in Python and further document to be applied for mathematical equations creating new notebooks, uploading the existing notebooks, import data from google drive etc., In this book the programs are worked in google colab. It also supports to Import/Publish notebooks from GitHub and also Import external datasets e.g. from Kaggle.

This book is compiled particularly during this pandemic mode to make coding and execution very simple to the learners so that the learners can compile and execute their codes online which in other case will be challenging and quite tough to install and work python application. Online education has become a viable and exciting method for instructional delivery and is a modern and innovative provider of e-learning course. Google Colab gives the right solution for this problem during this pandemic situation without any prerequisite setup and provides free access for computing resources including GPUs. It is a google research product which allows users to write, run and execute python code within the user's browser. This book is integrated with Python and Google Colab.

This book starts from the introduction and directs further focusing on small steps from the basics and covers varied topics that serve as a guide or tutorial to the fundamentals of Python programming. At the beginning of each chapter, the learning objectives is outlined that should be accomplished once you have gone through the chapter. Chapter 1 explains about the basic of python character set, tokens and simple programs. Chapter 2 discuss about operators and expressions. Chapter 3 focuses and explains about decision statements. Chapter 4 explains loop control statements. Chapter 5 describes about the types of function and its syntax, recursive and lambda functions. Chapter 6 is all about lists, tuples, sets and dictionaries. Chapter 7 and 8 explains the concepts of exception handling and file handling.

Authors Profile

Dr.N. Valliammal is working as Assistant Professor (SG) for Avinashilingam Institute for Home Science and Higher Education for Women from 2007 to till date. She received her Doctorate during 2014. To her credit she has published 6 Book Chapters and one chapter in Online Special Volume and also has compiled 4 Hand Books for Ancillary course offered to all the majors at University level. She has presented 13 papers in International Conferences. She has also published 24 articles in International Journals. Her area of interest includes Data Science, Data Analytics and Machine Learning. She has acted as a Content developer for Swayam - MooC Course - Cyber Security with four modules. She has also been appreciated as outstanding contributor for introducing ICT based teaching and learning methodology at University level certified by Spoken Tutorial IIT Bombay, 2021.

Dr.R. Vijayabhanu is a Assistant Professor (SG) in the Department of Computer Science at the Avinashilingam Institute for Home Science and Higher Education for Women of Coimbatore, where she received her PhD degree from the same Institution, in 2014. She has research background in Data Mining, Image Processing and Soft Computing and had compiled the ancillary book for the undergraduate students of the Institution and received appreciation. She has published 2 book chapters, 28 papers in International journals and presented 12 papers at International Conferences with a best paper award.

CHAPTER 1

1. Basic of Python

Learning Outcomes

- A brief introduction on Python Programming.
- Detailed illustrations on the Python Tokens.
- Python Data Types with Python programs.
- Study on assigning variables.
- Examples on Formatting in Python.
- Summarize Python Programs for Inbuilt Functions.

1.1. Introduction

A cross-platform programming language that can run on Windows, Mac-OS, Linux and which can be ported to Java and .Net. Python is a free, open-source, general purpose programming language which is case sensitive and interpretable.

Applications of Python

- Development of – Application, Web, Game, etc.
- System Administration.
- Scientific and Numbering Computing.
- GIS and Mapping.
- In Artificial Intelligence (AI) – Python has been developed in such a way to be great support for AI techniques. The framework, libraries and function are designed to efficiently improve the accuracy of AI methodologies. Thus coming in practical for speech recognition system, autonomous cars, interpreting data like images, patterns, videos, etc. The python libraries for Machine Learning – PyML, PyBrain, Neural Networks – PyAnn, Natural Language and Text Processing – Quepy, etc.
- In Big Data- Large data analyze has been successfully achieved by the Python. Some of the Python libraries for Big Data analysis are Pandas, NumPy, SciPy, IPython, Dask, etc.
- In Networking - Python has been proven to be cost-effective and the optimistic in networking tasks such as configuration of routers, read and write processes and automation works. Few built-in python libraries for networking are Netmiko, Paramiko SSH, PySNMP, NAPALM, etc.

Python is so Popular Because,

- A multiple programming prototype – including features such as object-oriented, imperative, procedural, functional, reflection, etc.

- Known for its large set of in-built library and tools.
- Takes simple format of commanding lines in comparison with the other popular programming languages such as C, C++ and Java.
- Very similar to Tel, Perl, Scheme or Java.
- Relatively useful as an extension language and stays as a remarkable support for the applications with programmable interface.

So Easy,

The text file such as a document or a notepad can be easily converted in to a python program by just saving them using the "**.py**" extension or using the command prompt of the python interface.

Eg: my_program.py.

With the internet facilities now-a-days, Python programming has become quite popular and uncomplicated with the promoted online compilers such as Pycharm, Spyder, Pythonany where and some web applications such as Google Colab. Google Co-laboratory commonly known as the Colab is an open source Jypyter notebook with cloud infrastructure which has been widely used in machine learning and deep learning applications.

Comments

In Python, the non-executed statement has been expressed using the comments beginning with the hash tags #.

Program No 1. Illustration on Comments

```
#Python Programming
#for
# the absolute beginner
print ("Hi Python")
```

Output

Hi Python

Why comments are used?

- Readable statements help in the future by referring at any particular part of a large program.
- Helps in collaboration of team members while working on a program to identify and understand.

1.2. Character Set

The set of characters enclosed within the square brackets are known as the **Character Set or Character Class** which is basically used to compare the characters of a provided string. The fundamental ASCII set of total codes registered on 0 to 127 are usually used to make up on a Python source file. But Python provides an exception of handling of external characters other than the usual ASCII codes to be used in a specific source file, perhaps only in the comments and strings commands.

While comparing with the set, every single character is considered irrespective of the order and the identical are returned as the results. The character set are also used during the specification of a certain range of characters. If the integers [0 – 9] is provided, the process is carried out by comparing each single digit between 0 and 9, which also goes for the case-sensitivity of alphabetic characters [a – z, A – Z].

1.3. Tokens

Each logical command in Python is broken into a progression of basic lexical compartments called the tokens. The basic **five tokens** explicitly used in the Python are: -

- Identifiers
- Keywords
- Delimiters
- Literals and
- Operators

1.3.1. Identifiers

The objects such as variables, functions, class, data structures, methods and modules are defined by using a character or letter known as identifiers. An identifier is made up of the alphabetic letters (A – Z, a –z), the numeric digits (0 – 9) and the underscore (_). They are expressed by either of the following ways in Python:

- Digits: 0 to 9
- Underscore:
- Alphabetic letters - Upper case: A to Z
                       - Lower case: a to z

  The identifier name in Python defines certain specifications like.
- With the Uppercase proceeded by lowercase (Myprogram) indicates that the identifier is quite a **conventional** type.

- With the single Underscore(_myprogarm) indicates that the identifier is a **Private** one.

- With the double Underscores (_myprogram) indicates that the identifier is **Firmly a Private**.

- When ends with the double Underscores (myprogram_) indicates that the identifier is a **Language – defined Special Name**.

  **Note: **Special characters such as @, $, etc are prohibited.

  ** Python being a case-sensitive language, 'A' and 'a' are consider conspicuously different.

1.3.2. Keywords

Python has reserved some of the words which are not used as the names of any identifiers. Being a case-sensitive programming language, the below keywords are used only with lower case. Some of the keywords are used to start some of the statements while the some are used only as the operators. There are 33 keywords in Python. The numbers may vary with different versions. All keywords except True, False and None are in lowercase.

Python Keywords

and	as	assert	pass	class	Continue	break	If	elif	For	except
del	in	false	from	global	Nonlocal	while	Or	else	Try	import
def	is	true	none	rasie	Lambda	yeild	not	with	Finally	return

Program No 2. Illustration on Keywords

    import keyword

    print(keyword.kwlist)

Output

['False', 'None', 'True', 'and', 'as', 'assert', 'async', 'await', 'break', 'class', 'continue', 'def', 'del', 'elif', 'else', 'except', 'finally', 'for', 'from', 'global', 'if', 'import', 'in', 'is', 'lambda', 'nonlocal', 'not', 'or', 'pass', 'raise', 'return', 'try', 'while', 'with', 'yield'].

1.3.3. Delimiters

Delimiters are the symbols basically used to provide the segregation of the various features and attributes of the Python comments. The symbols provide the identification of specific feature of the attribute and their functions. They differentiate the expressions as lists, tuple, dictionary, string, function, etc.

Various Delimiters

Braces	() {} []
Punctuations	, : . " " ' ' = ;
Assignment Operators	+= -= *= /= //= %=
	&= |= ^= >>= <<= **=
Others	# /

1.3.4. Literals

The strings and integers that are used while writing a Python program are collectively called as literals.

Program No 3. Illustration on Literals

```
[8]  3      #Integer Literal

     3


[10]
     9+0j    # Complex Literal

     (9+0j)


[11] 5.8    # Float Literal

     5.8


[12] "Literals"    # String literals"

     'Literals'


     """ Triple """    # Triple Quoted String

     ' Triple '
```

Thus using the above mentioned delimiters, literals and the operators, the programmers create Python programming statements and comments with the specific data types.

1.4. Python Data Type

Python basically adopts standard data types such as numbers, string and Boolean to store data in the memory.

1.4.1. Integers

The numeric integers can be of any length from –x to 0 to +x, where x = 0 – 9.

1.4.2. Floating Point Numbers

The decimal numbers such as 0.8, 98.67, ect belongs to the floating point numbers to which Python enhances accuracy up to 15 decimal points.

1.4.3. Complex Numbers

An order pair of real and imaginary values.

1.4.4. Boolean Type

Boolean values holds either TRUE or FALSE. The bool ( ) function has been used to evaluate or compare any value or expression to return either of above Boolean values as the result.

1.4.5. String Type

String is a set of characters in a contiguous form or a sequence, enclosed with the **quotation marks**. Single, double and even triple quotes are used.

Identifying the Data Type

The data type of an object in Python can be identified by using the **type ( ) function**.

Program No 4. Printing the Data Types Using type() Function

```
# Finding the data types using the type ( ) function
x = 6
y = 5.5
z = 1+0j
a = x < y
b = bool(7)
c = "color"
print("x = ", x , type(x))
print("y = ", y , type(y))
print("z = ", z , type(z))
print("a = ", a , type(a))
print("b = ", b , type(b))
print("c = ", c , type(c))
```

```
x =    6 <class 'int'>
y =    5.5 <class 'float'>
z =    (1+0j) <class 'complex'>
a =    False <class 'bool'>
b =    True <class 'bool'>
c =    color <class 'str'>
```

1.5. The Print ( ) Function

To display the program statement in the form of output, the print( ) function has been used.

Program No 5. Printing the String and the Integer Value

#To print a string

print ("We are printing a String Now !!!!")

Output

We are printing a String Now !!!!

To print an Integer Number

x=3

print(x)

Output

3

1.5.1. The Print ( ) Function with End Argument

The end is the parameter which has been used to consider a new line by default that following the print statement.

Program No 6. Printing Strings with End Arguments

```
# Pythun Programs N0 6.
# Printing with end arguments
print("Hi Guys!!!", end = ' ')
print("How are you???", end = '\n\n')
print("Bread", end = "&")
print("Butter", end = "")

Hi Guys!!! How are you???

Bread&Butter
```

1.6. Assigning a Value to a Variable

Python is the simplest and easiest programming language in comparison with other prominent languages such as C, C++ and Java. To store the value of an object, we use variables. In Python, there is no specific task like declaration of the variable.

For Example

In C:	In C++:

#include<studio.h>
int main( )
  {
int x =3;
printf ("Integer: %d", a);
  }
	#include<bits/stdc++.h>
	using namespace std;
	int main( )
	  {
	int x= 3;
	cout<<"Integer:" <<x;
	  }

But in **Python**,

```
x = 3
print("Integer: ",x)
```

Output

```
Integer: 3
```

A variable in the Python can be used to store a specific value of a data type. The value assignment to the variables are connected using the **'equal to ='** symbol.

```
x = 2
y = 4
z = x + y
print(z)
```

Output

```
6
```

```
# x, y, z are the variables
```

1.6.1. More on Assigning Values to a Variable

1. **Variable name:** The variable names can either begins with the alphabetic letters or underscore followed by characters and numeric digits.

Program No 7. Variable Names

```
a=5
print(a, "Type:", type(a))
_three=3
print(_three, "Type:", type(_three))
_99=99.98
print(_99, "Type:", type(_99))
program1="Python"
print(program1, "Type:", type(program1))
```

```
5 Type: <class 'int'>
3 Type: <class 'int'>
99.98 Type: <class 'float'>
Python Type: <class 'str'>
```

2. **Special Characters:** Any other special characters are prohibited.

3. **Case-sensitive:** As already known, Python considers "A" and "a" as completely discrete variables.

4. **Keywords:** The variable names can be of anything except the Python-defined keywords.

5. **No Space:** The variable names can be of any length, but empty space separation among the characters is not allowed. An underscore can be used instead.

my program="Python"

Error Output:

File "<ipython-input-17-2b60496db5c0>", line 1 my program="Python" ^

SyntaxError: invalid syntax

my_program="Python"
print(my_program)
output:
Python

1.6.2. Scope of Variable

The accessibility of the variable in a particular program is known as the Scope of the variable, according to which the variable is either consider as the **global** or the **local.**

The Global Variable

As the name goes, the global variable is used at any part of the program but has to be defined and declared before/outside of any function and does not specifically related to any function.

The Local Variable

The local variable is specified within a particular function and it can be called within that particular function only.

Program No 8. Global and Local Variables

```python
# Global and local variables
x = 10      #global variable
def addition():  # function
    y = 5      #local variable
    print("Sum of x + y = ",x+y)
addition()  # calling the function
```

```
Sum of x + y =  15
```

If we create a variable with the same name outside and inside of the function, the one inside the function acts as the local variable while the one outside the function acts as the global variable.

Program No 9. Global and Local Variables with Same Names

```
# Global and local variable with same name
x =10
def myadd():
  x=2
  print("Local variable x = ",x)
myadd()
print("Global variable x = ",x)


Local variable x =  2
Global variable x =  10
```

But to declare a global variable within a function, we use the ***global*** keyword in Python.

Program No 10. Program with Global Keyword

```
# Using global ( ) function
def myadd():
   global x
   x = 50
myadd()
y = 10
print ("Addition of x + y = ", x +y)

Addition of x + y =  60
```

1.7.   Multiple Assignments

Unlike other programming languages, Python programs are allowed to assign multiple variables in a single line, and same value to multiple variables.

- Assigning multiple variables with the same value. Eg: x = y = z = 5.
- Assigning multiple variables with multiple values. Eg: x, y, z = "Red", "Blue", "Green".

- x = y = z = 5
- print("x =",x)
- print("y =", y)
- print("z =", z)
- x, y, z ="Red", "Blue", "Green"
- print("x =",x)
- print("y =", y)
- print("z =", z)
- x = 5
- y = 5
- z = 5
- x = Red
- y = Blue
- z = Green

1.8. Writing Simple Program in Python

Program No 11. Simple Program to say "hi Python"

```python
# simple program to print "Hi Python" in two ways
print("Hi Python")          # simply with print() function
a = "Hi Python"             # declare the string
print(a)
```

```
Hi Python
Hi Python
```

Program No 12. Simple Program to Add Two Numbers

```python
# simple program  to add 2 numbers
x = 2
y = 5
print("Addition:", x+y)
   # or
z = x + y
print("Addition = ",z)
```

```
Addition: 7
Addition =  7
```

DIY Programs

1. Write a program to get the inputs from user in Python.
2. Write a program to check whether the given number is positive or negative.
3. Write a program to check the leap year.
4. Write a program to verify whether the character provided is a vowel or a consonant.
5. Write a program to know whether a number is odd or even and a prime number.

The Input ( ) Function

- The user input has been taken while executing the input ( ) function.
- The input ( ) function accepts the string values and but ever converts an integer value into a string.
- But to convert and make the integer and the other data types as the input, the **Typecasting** has been used.

1.8.1. Reading String ( ) from Console

```
Python 3.8.5 Shell                                                    —   □   X
File  Edit  Shell  Debug  Options  Window  Help
Python 3.8.5 (tags/v3.8.5:580fbb0, Jul 20 2020, 15:43:08) [MSC v.1926 32 bit (In
tel)] on win32
Type "help", "copyright", "credits" or "license()" for more information.
>>> |
```

- To read a string values from the console as an input to a Python program, the input ( ) function has been used.

- **What is a Console?**

Console termed as the shell in the Python Script, is simply a command line that has been used to get an input from the user.

- Every prompt command line on Python begins with '>>>' symbol.

- The commands are executed and interpreted at the same time by just pressing the 'ENTER' key.

Typecasting

The Type conversion is the process by which one data type has been converted to another manually. This conversion occurs in either of the following ways:

1. Implicit Conversion
2. Explicit Conversion

The Explicit type conversion is the process where Python-defined data types such as int, float and str are used. This is known as Typecasting done by consigning a specific data type function to an expression.

1. *Typecasting the Input to Integer*

Using the input ( ) function here, the Python gets an integer input from the programmer.

```python
x = int(input("Enter x value:"))
y = int(input("Enter y value:"))
z = x + y
print ("Sum of x and y:", z)
```

Output

    Enter x value:6

    Enter y value:9

    Sum of x and y: 15

2. *Typecasting the Input to Float*

A float value has been obtained from the programmer by the console using the float (input ( )).

    x = float(input("Enter x value:"))

    y = float(input("Enter y value:"))

    z = x + y

    print ("Sum of x and y:", z)

    Enter x value: 6.2

    Enter y value:5.2

    Sum of x and y: 11.4

3. *Typecasting the Input to String*

Irrespective of any other data type, the input ( ) considers it to be a string, possibly in typecasting the *str* keyword has been used.

    s = str(input("Enter a string:"))

    s1 = str(input("Enter an integer:"))

    s2 = str(input("Enter a float value:"))

    Enter a string: hello

    Enter an integer:8

    Enter a float value:6.3

1.9. The eval ( ) Function

The eval( ) is a command function that has been used to return an output value fora mentioned argument or expression.

Program No 13. Program with eval( ) function

```
# Eval () function program
x = 2
y = eval ("(x+4)*2")
z = eval ("(y+4)*2")
print("x  =  ", x)
print("y  =  ", y)
print("z  =  ", z)
print("x+y+z=", eval("x+y+z"))


x  =    2
y  =    12
z  =    32
x+y+z=  46
```

1.9.1. Apply eval ( ) to Input ( ) Function

Program No 14. Program with eval ( ) and Input( ) Functions

```
# Eval () and input ()
a = eval(input("Enter the values as an expression x + y:"))
b = eval(input("Enter the values as an expression x - y:"))
c = eval(input("Enter the values as an expression x * y:"))
print("x + y =  ", a)
print("x - y =  ", b)
print("x * y =  ", c)

Enter the values as an expression x + y:8+2
Enter the values as an expression x - y:8-2
Enter the values as an expression x * y:8*2
x + y =   10
x - y =   6
x * y =   16
```

1.10. Formatting Numbers and Strings

Formatting of numbers and string d goes in either of the two ways:

- Conventional method of using % operator and the data types.
- Using { } braces and format ( ) function.

Using % Operator and the Data Types

The % operator has been used in formatting of the Python codes with their specific data types.

- %i/%d   - Integers
- %f   - Floating values
- %s   - String
- %x   - Hex representation
- %c   - Single character
- %u   - Unsigned decimal integer
- %o   - Octal number

```python
# Conventional method of Formatting
print("Number: %d"%(5))  #Integer
print("Float: %f"%(5.0))  #Float
print("String: %s"%("Python")) #String
print("%c is a character" %("A")) #Single Character
print("%d converted into Octal: %02o"%(16,16))
print("%d converted into Octal: %04o"%(16,16))
print("%d converted into Hex: %02x"%(16,16))
print("%d converted into Hex: %04x"%(16,16))
```

Output

```
Number: 5
Float: 5.000000
String: Python
A is a character
16 converted into Octal: 20
16 converted into Octal: 0020
16 converted into Hex: 10
16 converted into Hex: 0010
```

Using { } Braces and Format ( ) Function

The curly braces are called as the placeholder that is used to hold indexes of string, number or an empty space.

Program No 15. Program with Format ( ) Function

```python
p = "Python"
print("This is a {} Program".format(p))
print("Program No:{}".format(15))
print("This is chapter {0} and Program No: {1}".format(1, 15))
print("Next chapter is {}".format(2))
```

```
This is a Python Program
Program No:15
This is chapter 1 and Program No: 15
Next chapter is 2
```

1.10.1. Formatting Floating Point Numbers

```
# Formatting Floating Point Number

# Using % operator

print("Float value: %f"%(2.76))

x = 4.5

print("The value of x = %f" %(x))

# Using Format() function

print("Float value: {:f}".format(2.9))

print("Float value: {}".format(2.9))

x = 9.999

print("Float value: {:f}".format(x))

print("Float value: {}".format(x))
```

Output

```
Float value: 2.760000

The value of x = 4.500000

Float value: 2.900000

Float value: 2.9

Float value: 9.999000

Float value: 9.999
```

1.10.2. Justifying Format

Functions to perform format justifiers are:

→ str. ljust(s, width[, fillchar]) for *Left Align*

→ str. rjust(s, width[, fillchar]) for *Right Align*

→ str. center(s, width[, fillchar]) for *Center Align*

- where s is the string.

The 'fillchar' argument may not be passed, since by default Python consider it as the empty space. But with the length and the specified 'fillchar' as parameters, the above functions are performed on the string to align them either to left or right or center. However, by justification string is not shorted either by losing its beginning or conclusion.

Program No 16. Program for Justifying Format

```python
#  Program for justifying format
s = "Python Programming"
print (s,"\n")
print (s.ljust (50), "\n")
print (s.center (50), "\n")
print (s.rjust (50), "\n")
print (s.center (25), "****************")
print (s.ljust (5), "****************")
print (s.rjust (30), "****************")
```

```
Python Programming

Python Programming

                    Python Programming

                              Python Programming

        Python Programming    ****************
Python Programming ****************
                Python Programming ****************
```

1.10.3. Integer Formatting

```python
# Formatting an Integer
# Using the % operator
print("Integer value: %d" %(67))
print("Integer value: %i" %(67))
print("Integer value: -%d" %(67))
print("Integer value: %d" %(-67))
x = -9
print("Integer value: %d" %(-x))
# Using Format() Function
print("Integer value: {}".format(34))
print("Integer value: {:d}".format(34))
print("Integer value: {}".format(-34))
x = -67
print("Integer value: {}".format(x))
print("Integer value: {}".format(-x))
```

Output

```
Integer value: 67
Integer value: 67
```

Integer value: -67

Integer value: -67

Integer value: 9

Integer value: 34

Integer value: 34

Integer value: -34

Integer value: -67

Integer value: 67

1.10.4. *String Formatting*

```python
# String Formatting
# Using % Operator
print("Name: %s"%("Python"))
print("Name: %s"%"Python")
print("Object: %s and Class: %s"%("Apple","Fruit"))
b = "Banana"
print("%s is a fruit"%b)
x = "fruit"
print("%s is a %s"%(b,x))
# Using Format() Function
print("Name: {}".format("Python"))
print("Name: {:s}".format("Python"))
print("Object: {0} and Class: {1}".format("Apple","Fruit"))
print("{} is a {}".format(b,x))
```

Output

Name: Python

Name: Python

Object: Apple and Class: Fruit

Banana is a fruit

Banana is a fruit

Name: Python

Name: Python

Object: Apple and Class: Fruit

Banana is a fruit

1.10.5. Formatting as a Percentage

To format a given number as percentage, *{:.n%}.format(num)* where n is the decimal for the percentage value and num is the number.

Program No 17. Program for Percentage Format

```
x = 0.50
y = -0.50
print("Percentage of x:" + "{:.2%}".format(x))
print("Percentage of y:" + "{:.2%}".format(y))
```

```
Percentage of x:50.00%
Percentage of y:-50.00%
```

```
a = 1/2
print("Percentage of a:" + "{:.0%}".format(a))
b = 1/3
print("Percentage of b:" + "{:.2%}".format(b))
```

```
Percentage of a:50%
Percentage of b:33.33%
```

1.10.6. Formatting Scientific Notation

- {.e} used on a number by str.format ( ) function to format that number to a scientific notation.
- To print the scientific notation of a number with specified number of digits, '{:.Ne}' has been used where N represents the number of digits.

```
x = "{:e}".format(12345)
print(x)
y = "{:.2e}".format(1000)
print(y)
```

Output

```
1.234500e+041.00e+03
```

1.11. Python In-built Functions

The instructions that are framed to accept the input and to do specific computational and execution processes in order to return the output is defined as the **Function**. In Python, there are:

- **In-built function:** Defined by the Python programming script.
- **User- defined function:** Declare by the user by omitting the Python keywords and are prefixed with '*def*'.

1. abs( )	18. enumerate( )	35. issubclass( )	52. range( )
2. all( )	19. eval( )	36. iter( )	53. repr( )
3. any( )	20. execu( )	37. len( )	54. reversed( )
4. ascii	21. filter( )	38. list( )	55. round( )
5. bin( )	22. float ( )	39. locals( )	56. set( )
6. bool( )	23. format( )	40.map( )	57. setatrr( )
7. bytearray( )	24. forzenset( )	41.max( )	58. slice( )
8. bytes( )	25. getattr( )	42. memoryview( )	59. sorted( )
9. callable( )	26. globals( )	43. min( )	60. str( )
10. chr( )	27. hasattr( )	44. next( )	61. sum( )
11. classmethod( )	28. hash( )	45. object( )	62. super( )
12. compile( )	29. help( )	46. oct ( )	63. tuple( )
13. complex ( )	30. hex( )	47. open( )	64. type( )
14. delattr( )	31. id( )	48. ord ( )	66. vars( )
15. dict( )	32. input( )	49. pow( )	67. zip(
16. dir( )	33. int ( )	50. print( )	68. @static method
17. divmod( )	34. isinstance( )	51. property( )	

1) abs( )

- ***Returns the exact value***

If the number provided is an integer or a floating point number, the absolute value will be returned. The magnitude value has been returned if complex number is provided.

```
>>> # abs()function
>>> abs(2)    # Integer
2
>>> abs(5.8)# float
5.8
>>> abs(2+6j) # complex
6.324555320336759
>>>
```

2) all ( )

- ### *True if All the Objects Are True*

The function use to return a Boolean value of TRUE, if the iterable objects are true, else FALSE.

```
# all() function
a = ("A", "B", "C")
print(all(a))
b = (1,0,0)
print(all(b))
```

```
True
False
```

3) any ( )

- ### *TRUE if Any of Objects are True*

If any of the iterable objects holds a true value, then a Boolean value of TRUE has been returned, else FALSE.

```
# any() function
a = ("", "A","")
print(any(a))
b = (0,0,0)
print(any(b))
```

```
True
False
```

4) ascii ( )

- ### *Readable Format of the Object*

To have the printable form of the given object, ascii ( ) function has been implemented.

```
# ascii() function
print(ascii("Python"))
print(ascii("pythön"))
print(ascii("äpplë"))
print(ascii("Apple"))
```

'Python'
'pyth\xf6n'
'\xe4ppl\xeb'
'Apple'

5) bin ( )

- ***Binary Conversion***

Bin() function converts an integer to a string of binary numbers(0,1). But float values are not interpreted.

```
# bin() function
print(bin(8))
x = 2
print(bin(x))
0b1000
0b10
```

6) bool ( )

- ***Boolean Conversion***

It returns either of the Boolean value, TRUE or FLASE of a specific object.

```
# bool() function
x = bool("Apple")
z = bool("")
k = bool(4.9)
print(x)
y = bool()
print(y)
print(z)
print(k)

True
False
False
True
```

7) bytearray ( )

- ### Array of Integers

The function returns a mutable sequence of integers in a form of an array.

```
# bytearray() function
a = bytearray(0)
print(a)
b = bytearray(1)
c = bytearray(2)
print(b)
print(c)
d = bytearray(3)
print(d)
bytearray(b'')
bytearray(b'\x00')
bytearray(b'\x00\x00')
bytearray(b'\x00\x00\x00')
```

8) bytes ( )

- ### Immutable Byte Objects

The immutable byte objects of the mentioned integers have been returned.

```
# bytes() function
a = bytes(0)
print(a)
b = bytes(3)
print(b)
c = bytes(5)
print(c)
d = bytes((1,2,3,4,5))
print(d)

b''
b'\x00\x00\x00'
b'\x00\x00\x00\x00\x00'
b'\x01\x02\x03\x04\x05'
```

9) callable ( )

- ### For Callable Objects

To check whether a specific object is callable, this particular function has been used and returns either TRUE or FLASE.

```
#callable() function
p = callable(1)
print(p)
q = callable("a")
print(q)
r = callable(callable)
print(r)
s = callable(list)
print(s)
False
False
True
True
```

10) chr ( )

- ### String for ASCII Value

The function returns a string value for the given integer value (ASCII value).

```
# chr() function
t = chr(65)
print(t)
u = chr(0)
print(u)
v = chr(6)
print(v)
w = chr(34)
print(w)
x = chr(101)
print(x)
A
�

"
e
```

11) classmethod ( )

- **Class Method of a Method**

The class method of a particular method has been returned by using this function.

```
# classmethod() function
class flower:
 n = 3
  def rose(color):
    print("RED rose of",color.n)
flower.rose = classmethod(flower.rose)
flower.rose()


RED rose of 3
```

12) compile ( )

- **Execution Command**

The function works as the command function to execute the given arguments or expressions and returns the code object.

```
#compile() function
x = 5
calculate = compile('x+2','test','single')
print("Addition: ")
calculate = compile('x-2','test','single')
print("\nSubration:")
calculate = compile('x*2','test','single')
exec(calculate)
exec(calculate)
print("\nMultiplication:")
exec(calculate)
Addition:
7

Subration:
3

Multiplication:
10
```

13) complex ( )

- ***Complex Number***

A complex is made up of a real value and an imaginary value [x+yj]. Thus, complex () returns the x+yj numbers where x and y can be integers or float values.

```
# complex() function
a = complex(2,3)
print(a)
b = complex(4,0)
print(b)
c = complex(3.8,4)
print(c)
d = complex(8, 2.3)
print(d)
 (2+3j)
(4+0j)
(3.8+4j)
(8+2.3j)
```

14) delattr ( )

- ***Delete the Attribute***

To have a change in the given attributes of an object, the delattr() is used.

```
# delattr() function
class flower:
  size = 6
  color = "Red"
  petals =35
rose = flower()
rose.size
delattr(flower,"size")
```

15) dict ( )

- ***Dictionary***

To create a dictionary which is one of the standard Python data type, the dict ( ) has been executed.

```python
#dict() function
i = dict(((0,1), (2,3),(4,5)))
j = dict([("Apple","Fruit"),("Rose", "Flower")])
print(i)
print(j)


{0: 1, 2: 3, 4: 5}
{'Apple': 'Fruit', 'Rose': 'Flower'}
```

16) dir ( )

- ### List of Local Attributes

The local attributes of an object has been returned in form of a list by performing this function.

```python
# dir() function
class flower:
 size = 6
 color = "Red"
 petals = 35
rose = flower()
dir(rose)
['_class_',
'_delattr_',
'_dict_',
'_dir_',
'_doc_',
'_eq_',
'_format_',
'_ge_',
'_getattribute_',
'_gt_',
'_hash_',
'_init_',
'_init_subclass_',
```

     '__le__',
     '__lt__',
     '__module__',
     '__ne__',
     '__new__',
     '__reduce__',
     '__reduce_ex__',
     '__repr__',
     '__setattr__',
     '__sizeof__',
     '__str__',
     '__subclasshook__',
     '__weakref__',
     'color',
     'petals',
     'size']

17) divmod ( )

- ### *Quotient and Reminder*

The division results of quotient and the reminder of two members are returned while performing this function.

```
# divmod() function
a = divmod(3,9)
print(a)
b = divmod(9,3)
print(b)
c = divmod(5,2.5)
print(c)
d = divmod(14.9, 7.8)
print(d)
 (0, 3)
(3, 0)
(2.0, 0.0)
(1.0, 7.1000000000000005)
```

18) Enumerate ( )

- **Enumerate Object**

An enumerate object has been returned through this function. The enumerated object is the opposite of the iterable objects.

```
# enumerate() function
for x in enumerate(["a","b","c"]):
  print("Enumerate Objects are:\n",x)
Enumerate Objects are:
 (0, 'a')
Enumerate Objects are:
 (1, 'b')
Enumerate Objects are:
 (2, 'c')
```

19) eval ( )

- **Evaluate**

It is a command function which returns the output of the mentioned arguments or expressions.

```
# eval() function
x= 5
print(eval('x+2'))
a = "Python"
b = "Programming"
print("Book:", eval('a+b'))
7
Book: PythonProgramming
```

20) execu ( )

- **Execution**

It is a command function to execute the arguments provided within the function.

```
#exec() function
exec('a =3; b=5; print(a+b)')
exec('x = 2; y = 8; print(x*y)')
8
16
```

21) filter ( )

- ***True Valued Attributes are Filtered***

The items of a particular function with hold the TRUE Boolean value or those who passes the condition are filtered using this function.

```
# filter() function
a = [ 1,2,3,4,5,6,7,8,9,10]
x1 = list(filter(lambda x:x%2 !=0,a))
print("x1 =",x1)
x2 = list(filter(lambda x:x%2 ==0,a))
print("x2 =", x2)
x1 = [1, 3, 5, 7, 9]
x2 = [2, 4, 6, 8, 10]
```

22) float ( )

- ***Floating Point Number***

To have a float value of a particular integer, the float () function has been implemented.

```
# float() function
a = float(4)
print(a)
b = float(-9)
print(b)
c = float(+43)
print(c)
4.0
-9.0
43.0
```

23) format ( )

- ***Formatting***

This function helps to format a specified value, mainly used with the strings.

```
# format() function
print("{} ia my country". format("India"))
print("{0} +{1} = {2}". format(3,1,4))

India ia my country
3 +1 = 4
```

24) frozenset ( )

- **Return of Immutable Frozen Set**

Every immutable frozen set are returned using this function.

```
# formatset() function
a = frozenset({4,3,5,2,1})
print(a)
b = frozenset({"a","d","b","c"})
print(b)
frozenset({1, 2, 3, 4, 5})
frozenset({'b', 'a', 'd', 'c'})
```

25) getattr ( )

- **Acquire Attributes**

To have a specific attribute value of an object, getattr () is used.

```
# getattr() function
class flower:
  size = 6
  color = "Red"
  petals = 35
rose = flower()
rose.size
s = getattr(rose, "size")
c = getattr(rose,"color")
print("Size = ",s)
print("Color = ",c)
p = getattr(rose,"petals")
print("Petals = ",p)
Size =  6
Color =  Red
Petals =  35
```

26) hasattr ( )

- **Check Whether the Attribute is in the Class**

The hasattr ( ) is used to know whether an attribute is present within an object.

```python
# hasattr() function
class flower:
    size = 6
    color = "Red"
    petals = 35
rose = flower()
rose.size
s = hasattr(rose, "size")
print("Size = ",s)
c = hasattr(rose,"color")
print("Color = ",c)
p = hasattr(rose,"petals")
print("Petals = ",p)

Size =  True
Color =  True
Petals =  True
```

27) hash ( )

- ### Hash Value

Every object in Python holds a hash value. The hash() function returns those hash values.

```python
# hash() function
a = hash(78)
print(a)
b = hash(-78)
print(b)
print(hash("Python"))
print(hash("python"))
print(hash(0))
print(hash(hash))
78
-78
-5869112512550032027
3991152322880351388
0
2920056221406
```

28) help ( )

- ***Aid***

Being an user-friendly programming language, the Python aids the programmer with the help () function. The function provides the list of modules, keywords, symbols or topics.

```
#help() function
help()
```

Welcome to Python 3.7's help utility!

If this is your first time using Python, you should definitely check out the tutorial on the Internet at https://docs.python.org/3.7/tutorial/.

Enter the name of any module, keyword, or topic to get help on writing Python programs and using Python modules. To quit this help utility and return to the interpreter, just type "quit".

To get a list of available modules, keywords, symbols, or topics, type "modules", "keywords", "symbols", or "topics". Each module also comes with a one-line summary of what it does; to list the modules whose name or summary contain a given string such as "spam", type "modules spam".

You are now leaving help and returning to the Python interpreter.

If you want to ask for help on a particular object directly from the interpreter, you can type "help(object)". Executing "help('string')" has the same effect as typing a particular string at the help> prompt.

```
help>
```

29) hex ( )

- ***Hexadecimal Value***

The give value has been renovated into a hexadecimal value, prefixed with '0x' by this function.

```
# hex() function
print(hex(6))
print(hex(-8))
print(hex(11))
print(hex(65))
print(hex(1001))
0x6
-0x8
0xb
0x41
0x3e9
```

30) id ( )

- ***Identity***

This function returns the identity of an object.

```
# id() function
print(id(1))
print(id("a"))
print(id("A)"))
print(id(1.7))
93959637486080
139683625129456
139682931462896
139682931139984
```

31) input ( )

- ***Display***

To input the program using a line of string by the user or to command for an input, the input()
function is used.

```
# input() function
int(input("Enter an integer:"))
str(input("Enter a string:"))
float(input("Enter a float value:"))
Enter an integer:25
Enter a string:Python
Enter a float value:50.3
50.3
```

32) int ( )

- ***Interger***

To convert a given value into an integer the above function is executed.

```
# int() function
print(int(3.8))
print(int(-99))
print(int(-3.7))
print(int(+8))
3
-99
-3
8
```

33) isinstance ( )

- ### *Check Whether an Object Belongs to the Class*

With a variable and a class as the arguments, the isinstance() function returns the Boolean value of TRUE if the variable belongs that particular mentioned class, else FALSE.

```
# isinstance() function
x = 54
print("Data type of x is Integer???", isinstance(x, int))
y = "Python"
print("Data type of y is String???", isinstance(y, str))
z = 8.9
print("Data type of z is Integer???", isinstance(z,int))
Data type of x is Integer??? True
Data type of y is String??? True
Data type of z is Integer??? False
```

34) issubclass ( )

- ### *Subclass of a Class*

To verify is an exacting class is a subclass of an another class, issubclass() function has been used. Two arguments of a major class and a subclass will be given within the function where the Boolean value of TRUE or FALSE has been received accordingly.

```
# issubclass() function
class flower:
 pass
class rose(flower):
 pass
a = issubclass (rose, flower)
print(a)
b = issubclass(flower,rose)
print(b)
True
False
```

35) iter ( )

- ### *Iterator*

To have the iterators of a particular object, the iter ( ) function has been used.

```
# iter() function
for i in iter([1,2,3,4]):
  print(i)
1
2
3
4
```

36) len ( )

- ### *Object Length*

The length of an object is known through this function.

```
#len() function
print(len((1,2,3,4,5)))
print(len("Python"))
print(len({"a","b","c","d","e"}))
print(len([1,2,2,3]))
5
6
5
4
```

37) list ( )

- ### *List –Data Type*

The list( ) function creates a sequence of values separated with comas and are enclosed within the square brackets '[ ]'.

```
# list() function
print(list((1,2,3,4,5)))
print(list(("a","b","c","d","e")))
print(list((2.1,2.3,3.4,5.6)))
[1, 2, 3, 4, 5]
['a', 'b', 'c', 'd', 'e']
[2.1, 2.3, 3.4, 5.6]
```

38) locals( )

- ***Local Symbol Table***

  The function will return a dictionary of the existing and updated local symbol table.

```
>>> # locals() function
>>> locals()
{'__name__': '__main__', '__doc__': None, '__package__': None, '__loader__': <cl
ass '_frozen_importlib.BuiltinImporter'>, '__spec__': None, '__annotations__': {
}, '__builtins__': <module 'builtins' (built-in)>}
>>>
```

39) map ( )

- ***Maps an Object***

The function maps the particular object with iterator and returns the corresponding Boolean values as the results.

```
# map() function
list(map(lambda x:x%2 == 0, [1,2,3,4,5]))
 [False, True, False, True, False]
```

40) max ( )

- ***Maximum Value***

During the iteration, the largest value has been identified by using this function.

```
# max() function
print(max((2,3,1,5,4)))
print(max(("b","d","r","s","a")))
print(max((3.2,4.3,4.2,7.3,2.3,1.0)))
5
s
7.3
```

41) memoryview ( )

- ***Memory Location***

The argument's memory has been shared by this function.

```
# memoryview() function
x = bytes(5)
for i in memoryview(x):
  print(i)
0
0
0
0
0
```

42) min ( )

- ***Minimum Value***

During the iteration, the least value has been identified by using this function.

```
# min() function
print(min((2,3,1,5,4)))
print(min(("b","d","r","s","a")))
print(min((3.2,4.3,4.2,7.3,2.3,1.0)))
1
a
1.0
```

43) next ()

- ***Next Item***

The function identifies the next item in the iteration.

```
# next() function
x = iter([1,2,3,4,5])
print(next(x))
print("the next .....")
next(x)
1
the next .....
2
```

44) object ( )

- ***Empty Object***

The function creates an empty object.

```
# object() function
x = object()
print(type(x))
print(dir(x))
<class 'object'>
['__class__','__delattr__','__dir__','__doc__','__eq__','__format__','__ge__','__getattribute__',
'__gt__','__hash__','__init__','__init_subclass__','__le__','__lt__','__ne__','__new__',
'__reduce__','__reduce_ex__','__repr__','__setattr__','__sizeof__','__str__',
'__subclasshook__']
```

45) oct ( )

- ***Octal Number***

The function is for the octal conversion of a number and provides the octal results prefixed with '0o'.

```
# oct() function
print(oct(6))
print(oct(16))
print(oct(-7))
print(oct(65))
print(oct(1001))
0o6
0o20
-0o7
0o101
0o1751
```

46) open ( )

- ***Open File***

Python allows us to open a saved file using this function.

```
# open() function
a = open("hi_python.py")
print(a)
```

47) ord ( )

- ***ASCII- Integer***

The function returns an integer value for a given Unicode value. In other words, gives ASCII value for the given character.

```
# ord() function
print(ord("a"))
print(ord("A"))
print(ord("9"))
print(ord("$"))
97
65
57
36
```

48) pow ( )

- ### *Power of a Number*

a^b = pow(a,b)

The pow() function is used to find the power of a number by providing the number and its power value within the function.

```
# pow() function
print(pow(2,3))
print(pow(-2,3))
print(pow(3,2))
print(pow(-3,2))
print(pow(3.7,-3))
8
-8
9
9
0.019742167295125655
```

49) print ( )

- ### *To Print*

The print () function works as the output command function.

```
# print() function
print("Hi, Python")
x =1
print(x)
a = 2
b = 3
print(a+b)
print("Addition of a and b is", a+b)
Hi, Python
1
5
Addition of a and b is 5
```

50) Property ( )

- ### Attribute Property

Each attribute of class holds their own unique property. This function returns those properties of the specified Python entity.

```
class flower:
  def _init_ (self, rose):
    self._rose = rose
  def get_rose(self):
    print("Getting rose")
    return self._rose
  def set_rose(self, value):
    print("Setting rose to " + value)
    self._rose = value
  def del_rose(self):
    print("Deleting rose")
    del self._rose
  rose = property (get_rose, set_rose, del_rose,'Name property')
p = flower('WHITE')
print(p.rose)
p.rose = 'RED'

del p.rose
```

51) range ( )

- ### Range

A sequence of numbers probably starting with 0 and ascends by 1 as to the extent of the provided argument is defined as the range.

```
# range() function
print(list(range(0)))
print(range(5))
print(list(range(5)))
print(list(range(3,8)))
print(list(range(7,2,-7)))
print(list(range(-5,5)))
[]
range(0, 5)
[0, 1, 2, 3, 4]
[3, 4, 5, 6, 7]
[7]
[-5, -4, -3, -2, -1, 0, 1, 2, 3, 4]
```

52) repr ( )

- ### *Represented String*

The function returns the readable format of the represented string.

```
# repr() function
print(repr("Python"))
print(repr(7))
print(repr(0x23))
print(repr(0o45))

'Python'
7
35
37
```

53) reversed ( )

- ### *Reverse an Item*

The function works to reverse an iterable object.

```
# reversed() function
x = reversed([5,4,3,2,1])
for i in x:
  print(i)
1
2
3
4
5
```

54) round ( )

- ### *Round-off Value*

The function returns an integer value for a floating point value. But to have a float value instead, the number of digits can be mentioned as the second argument.

```
# round() function
print(round(8.9))
print(round(-5.4))
print(round(9.756546,2))
print(round(9.0,4))
9
-5
9.76
9.0
```

55) set ( )

- ### Set of Items

The function provides us the set of items of an object within the set brackets { }.

```
# set() function
print(set((1,2,3,4,5)))
print(set(["a","b","c"]))
print(set([1,2,3,3,4,5,5]))


{1, 2, 3, 4, 5}
{'b', 'a', 'c'}
{1, 2, 3, 4, 5}
```

56) Setattr ( )

- ### Alter an Attribute

The setattr () has been used to set or change the value of an attribute of a particular class.

```
class flower:
  size = 6
  color = "Red"
  petals = 35
rose = flower()
c = getattr(rose,"color")
print("Color = ",c)
setattr(rose,"color", "White")
print("Now the color is ....")
rose.color
```

57) slice ( )

- ### Crop

With the specified range (start, stop, step) value , a set of indices are chopped off from a string value.

```
# slice() function
print("Python"[slice(1,5,2)])
print("Python"[slice(0,5,3)])
print("Python"[slice(2,5,3)])
print("Python"[slice(1,6,2)])
yh
Ph
t
yhn
```

58) sorted( )

- ### *Sorted Order of Given List*

The sorted () function as the name goes provides us a sorted format of the given list.

```
# sorted() function
print(sorted((2,3,1,5,4)))
print(sorted(["b","d","r","s","a"]))
print(sorted((3.2,4.3,4.1,7.3,2.3,1.0)))
[1, 2, 3, 4, 5]
['a', 'b', 'd', 'r', 's']
[1.0, 2.3, 3.2, 4.1, 4.3, 7.3]
```

59) str ( )

- ### *String*

To convert a given value into a string the above function is executed.

```
# str() function
print(str(7))
print(str("Python"))
print(str('True'))
print(str("|"))
print(str([1,2,3]))
7
Python
True
|
[1, 2, 3]
```

60) sum ( )

- ### *Addition*

The sum of two arguments has been returned as the result through this function. The arguments here are considered as the iterables.

```
# sum() function
print(sum((1,2,3),4))
print(sum([1,2,3,4,5],2))
print(sum({2,4,6,8},10))
10
17
30
```

61) super ( )

- ***Parent class***

The function helps us to get the parent class.

```
# super() function
class Python:
  def _init_ (self):
    print("Chapter: 1")
class Chapter:
  def _init_ (self):
    super()._init_()
    print("Built-in Functions")
```

62) tuple ( )

- ***Tuple – Data Type***

The tuple ( ) function creates a sequence of values separated with comas and are enclosed within the curved brackets '( )'.

```
# tuple() function
print(tuple((2,3,1,5,4)))
print(tuple(["b","d","r","s","a"]))
print(tuple((3.2,4.3,4.1,7.3,2.3,1.0)))
 (2, 3, 1, 5, 4)
('b', 'd', 'r', 's', 'a')
(3.2, 4.3, 4.1, 7.3, 2.3, 1.0)
```

63) type ( )

- ***Data Type***

To verify the data type of a particular object in Python, the type () function has been used.

```
# type() function
x = 12
print(type(x))
print(type(3.14))
print(type(2+8j))
print(type("Python"))
a = object()
print(type(a))
<class 'int'>
<class 'float'>
<class 'complex'>
<class 'str'>
<class 'object'>
```

64) vars ( )

- ### *Variables*

The function helps us to know the _dict_property of the object.

```
# vars() function

class flower:

  size = 6

  color = "Red"

  petals = 35

vars(flower)

mappingproxy({'_dict_': <attribute '_dict_' of 'flower' objects>,

        '_doc_': None,

        '_module_': '_main_',

        '_weakref_': <attribute '_weakref_' of 'flower' objects>,

        'color': 'Red',

        'petals': 35,

        'size': 6})
```

65) zip ( )

- ### *Concatenate*

To link or join two or more iterators into a single iterator, this function is used.

```
# zip() function

print(set(zip([1,2,3],["a","b","c"])))

print(set(zip(["Python","Chapter"],["Programming",1])))

{(1, 'a'), (2, 'b'), (3, 'c')}

{('Python', 'Programming'), ('Chapter', 1)}
```

66) @static Method ( )

- ### *Static Method*

To produce a static method by using function called @static method ().

```
# staticmethod() function
class python:
  def chapter():
    print("Frist chapter")
python.chapter = staticmethod(python.chapter)
python.chapter()

Frist chapter

class first:
  @staticmethod
  def intro():
    print("Hi, Python")
first.intro()
Hi, Python
```

1.11.1. *The ord and chr Functions*

The ord() function is a complementary function of chr() function. The ord() returns the integer ASCII value for the provided String ASCII value while the chr() does the exact opposite by returning an ASCII string for ASCII integer.

```
# ord() function
Ord("A")
65
Ord("a")
97
Ord("6")
54
Ord("\n")
10
Ord("^")
94
Ord("65")
A
```

Summary

In this chapter, you have learned about Python and its strength. Also you have discussed various data types and how to work with them. You learned about variables and how to store and retrieve information. You also know how to format numbers and Strings as well as python in-built functions. Finally, you learned how to get user input to make your programs interactive.

References

[1]   https://www.python.org/

[2]   www.tutorialspoint.com

[3]   www.upgrad.com

[4]   www.realpython.com

[5]   www.geeksforgeeks.org

[6]   www.iteanz.com

[7]   www.learnpython.org

1.12. Test Your Skill

Multiple Choice Questions

1. Which is a cross-platform programming language that can run on Windows, Mac-OS, Linux and which can be ported to Java and .Net?

    a) C

    b) C++

    c) Python

    d) R

2. Python is an open-source general purpose programming language which is _____________

    a) Case sensitive and interpretable

    b) Case sensitive and uninterpretable

    c) Non-case sensitive and interpretable

    d) Non-case sensitive and uninterpretable.

3. What are the Python libraries available for Big Data analysis?

    a) Pandas

    b) IPython

    c) NumPy, Scipy

    d) All of the above

4. In Python, the non-executed statement has been expressed using the comments beginning with ____________

   a) /

   b) //

   c) #

   d) *

5. The set of characters enclosed within the square brackets is known as ____________

   a) Character Set

   b) Character collection

   c) Character list

   d) String

6. Each logical command in Python is broken into a progression of basic lexical compartments called ____________

   a) Variables

   b) Tokens

   c) Lexicon

   d) Expressions

7. ____________are the symbols basically used to provide the segregation of the various features and attributes of the Python comments.

   a) Variables

   b) Delimiters

   c) Literals

   d) Characters

8. The process by which manually converting one data type to another is called ____________

   a) Type Conversion

   b) Typesetting

   c) Data Conversion

   d) Data Casting

9. The ____________ variable is specified within a particular function and it can be called within that particular function only.

   a) Global

   b) Local

   c) Internal

   d) Static

10. Which of the following is not a keyword in python?

   a) Assert

   b) Lambda

   c) Val

   d) In

Review Questions

1. List some features of Python.
2. Give the rules for naming an identifier in Python.
3. How can you give comments in Python?
4. What are the data types available in Python?
5. List some built-in functions in Python.

CHAPTER 2

2. Operators and Expressions

Learning Outcomes

- Depict the Python Operators, its types and Expressions.
- Illustrate Arithmetic Operators in Python.
- Importance of Operator Precedence and Associativity.
- Illustrate Bitwise Operators and types.

2.1.   Introduction

The technical programmings are the extended domain of the modern technological world. The computational intelligence has been governed by the programs that justify the mathematical, logical and reasonable evaluations. Such computations and processes are based on the inputs and methodological features to provide the optimistic outcomes. The computational processes are done using the **operations and expressions**. The operation is the evaluation process by using one or more operands with a specific operator to return a value as the result while an expression is the logical progression of operators and operands.

2.2.   Operators and Expression

Arithmetic and logical calculations are done using the operators and operands. There are seven types of built-in operators in Python:-

1.   **Arithmetic Operators** - +, -, *, /, Modules (%), Exponent (**), Floor Division (//).
2.   **Assignment Operators** – Equal (=), Add AND (+=).
3.   **Bitwise Operators**- Manipulate with bits and performs bit-by- bit operations.
4.   **Comparison (Relational) Operators**- Generally works like a control statement, and returns either TRUE or FALSE based on the condition provided.
5.   **Identity Operators**- For comparing memory locations of two objects (is, is not).
6.   **Logical Operators** – OR, AND, NOT.
7.   **Membership Operators**- in, not in.

1. Arithmetic Operators: Here consider x = 6 and y = 2.

1.	Addition (+)	a = x + y	a=x+y: 8
2.	Subtraction (-)	b = x - y	b=x-y: 4
3.	Multiplication (*)	c = x * y	c=x*y: 12
4.	Division (/)	d = x / y	d=x/y: 3.0
5.	Modules (%)	e = x % y	e=x%y: 0
6.	Exponent (**)	f = x ** y	f=x**y: 36
7.	Floor Division (//)	g=x//y	g=x//y: 3

2. Assignment Operators: Consider a = 5and b = 2.

Addition	c = a + b	Adds a, b and assigns to c	**c= a+b: 7**
Add AND	c += a	Equivalent to c = c +a	**c+=a: 12**
Subtract AND	c -= a	Equivalent to c = c –a	**c-=a: 7**
Multiply AND	c*= a	Equivalent to c = c *a	**c*=a: 35**
Divide AND	c /= a	Equivalent to c = c /a	**c /=a: 7.0**
Modules AND	c %= a	Equivalent to c = c %a	**c%=a: 2.0**
Floor Division	c //= a	Equivalent to c = c //a	**c //= a: 0.0**
Exponent	c **= a	Equivalent to c = c **a	**c **=a: 0.0**
AND	c &= a	Equivalent to c = c & a	**c &= a: 0**
OR	c |= a	Equivalent to c = c | a	**c /= a: 5**
NOT	c ^= a	Equivalent to c = c ^a	**c ^= a: 0**

3. Comparison Operators: Here a = 5 and b = 10.

8.	=	2 operands should be equal if not FALSE	a == b	Is a==b?: False
9.	!=	2 operands not equal, then TRUE	a!= b	Is a!=b ?: True
10.	>	Left operand should be greater than right, then TRUE	a > b	Is a > b?: False
11.	<	Left operand should not be greater than right, then TRUE	a < b	Is a<b?: True
12.	>=	Left operand should be greater than or equal to the right, then TRUE	a >= b	Is a >= b?: False
13.	<=	Left operand should not be greater than or equal to the right, then TRUE	a <= b	Is a <= b?: True

4. Logical Operator: Here values of a, b and c are taken as 6, 3, and 0 respectively.

14.	Logical AND	If both operands are true, then true	a AND b	**Is a < 9 and a> 2? True** **Is b < 2 and b > 9? False**
15.	Logical OR	Any of the operands are non-zero, then true	a OR b	**Is a < 2 OR a > 4? True** **Is b < 2 OR b > 4? True**
16.	Logical NOT	To reverse the logical state of its operand	NOT a	**NOT of a: False** **NOT of c: True**

5. Identity Operators: Say `x = [ "Pencil", "Pen", "Ruler" ]`, `z = x` and `y = [ 'Pencil', 'Pen', 'Ruler' ]`

17.	Is	Returns TRUE if the variables x and y shares the same location on the memory, else FALSE	id(x) = id(y), then 1	`Whether x IS y? : False` `Whether x IS z? : True`
18.	Is not	Returns TRUE if the variables x and y does not shares the same location on the memory, else FALSE	id(x) != id(y), then 1	`Whether x IS NOT y? : True` `Whether x IS NOT z? : False`

6. Bitwise Operators: Let us have a as 5 while b as 2.

19.	Binary AND	&	a & b	`c = a & b : bin ( c) = 0b0`
20.	Binary OR	|	a | b	`c = a | b : bin ( c) = 0b111`
21.	Binary XOR	^	a ^ b	`c = a ^ b : bin ( c) = 0b111`
22.	Ones' Complement	~	~ a	`c = ~a  : bin ( c) = -0b110`
23.	Binary Left Shift	<<	a << b	`c = a << b : bin ( c) = 0b10100`
24.	Binary Right Shift	>>	a >> b	`c = a >> b : bin ( c) = 0b1`

7. Membership Operators: Consider a= [1, 3, 5, 7, 9] and b = [2, 4, 6, 8].

25.	in	TRUE when a variable is in the specified sequence or FALSE	x in a	`Is 1 in a ? : True` `Is 1 in b ? : False`
26.	not in	TRUE when a variable is not in the specified sequence or FALSE	x not in a	`Is 2 not in a ? : True` `Is 2 not in b ? : False`

Statements & Expressions

The logical instructions are read and executed by the Python Interpreter through either an expression or an assignment statement.

- A statement is defines the way an expression crates objects and preserve them.
- An Expression is a logical sequence of numbers, strings, objects, functions and operators. All mathematical and logical operations are performed using the expression.

Eg: Using a simple arithmetic expression.

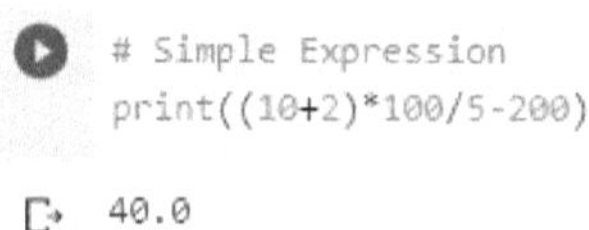

- **Simple Assignment Statement**: used to assign new variables and change the values.

- **Augmented Assignment Statement**: used to combine various arithmetic operators.
  Eg: a = x + y

- **Multi-line Statement:** by using the line continuation character (\).

Explicit Line Continuation	Implicit Line Continuation
Using \ to split a statement into multiple lines. Eg:-	Split a statement using either of parentheses ( ), brackets [ ] and braces { }. Eg:-

```
>>> my_list = [ 1,\
          2,3\
          ,4,5]
>>> print (my_list)
[1, 2, 3, 4, 5]
>>> eval(\
      "2.5\
+3.5")
6.0
>>> |
```

```
>>> result = (10+100
          *5-5
          /100+10
          )
>>> print ( result)
519.95
>>> |
```

2.3. Arithmetic Operators

The basic mathematic calculations such as Addition, Subtraction, Multiplication and Division are performed using the Arithmetic operators. They are includes computation of Floor Division, Exponent and Modulus.

2.3.1. Binary Operators

When the operation is performed by using two operands and an operator, then it is known as Binary operator. In Python, the binary arithmetic operators are, 11[2].

- Addition **(+)**
- Subtraction **(-)**
- Multiplication **(*)**
- Division **(/)**
- Modules **(%)**
- Exponent **(**)**
- Floor Division **(//)**

Program 2.1 Arithmetic Binary Operations

```
# Program for Arithmetic Binary Operators
x = 11
y = 2
a = x + y      # Addition using "+" operator
b = x - y      # Subtraction using "-" operator
c = x * y      # Multiplication using "*" operator
d = x / y      # Division using "/" operator
e = x % y      # Modulus using "%" operator
f = x ** y     # Exponent using "**" operator
g = x // y     # Floor Division using "//" operator
print("Addition using + operator:   ", a)
print("Subtraction using - operator: ",b)
print("Multiplication using * operator: ",c)
print("Division using / operator: ",d)
print("Modulus using % operator: ", e)
print("Exponent using ** operator: ",f)
print("Floor Division using // operator: ",g)
```

```
Addition using + operator:   13
Subtraction using - operator:  9
Multiplication using * operator:  22
Division using / operator:  5.5
Modulus using % operator:  1
Exponent using ** operator:  121
Floor Division using // operator:  5
```

2.3.2. Unary Operators

The operator takes a single operand to perform an operation; such operators are known as Unary operator. The unary operators are "minus -" (negative), "plus+" (positive) and "invert ~" (complement).

- Unary - operator: The contrary value for a numeric value has been computed.
- Unary + operator: The actual value has been returned.
- Unary ~ operator: This works only with the integers and as the complementary conversion.

```
# Program for Arithmetic Unary Operators
a = 2
print("Unary - operator with operand a: ",-a)
print("Unary + operator with operand a:   ",  +a)
print("Unary ~ operator with operand a: ",~a)
```

```
Unary - operator with operand a:   -2
Unary + operator with operand a:   2
Unary ~ operator with operand a:   -3
```

2.4.   Operator Precedence and Associativity

Let's consider an expression **10*2 +5 =?**By evaluating this expression we might get **25**(10*2+5 = 20+5) and **70**(10*2+5 = 10*7) as the results. But the expression should have only one valid answer; thereby we have to decide the operation sequence like which operation either addition or multiplication should be performed first. Thus, to overcome this sort of situation the operation precedence has been declared in Python.

Operation Precedence is the declaration of ordering or prioritizing of the operators' execution sequence. Python separates the operators into two order of precedence,

- **Highest precedence operators** – Yields the highest priority of execution.
- **Lowest precedence operators** – Yields the lowest priority or executed as the last part of computation.

Highest Precedence	Lowest Precedence
1. Parentheses ( )	10. Bitwise XOR ^
2.List and Dictionary [ ], { }	11. Bitwise OR|
3. Function calls, Referring Attributes, Slicing	12. Comparison, Identity and Membership operators <, >, <=,>=,!=, ==, in, notin, is, isnot
4. Exponent **	
5. Unary Operators +,-,~	13. Boolean NOT not
6. Multiplication, Division, Floor Division, Modulus *,/, //, %	14. Boolean AND and
	15. Boolean OR or
7. Addition, Subtraction +,-	16. Conditional statement if...else
8. Left and Right Shifts <<, >>	17. Lambda lambda
9. Bitwise AND &	18. Assignment expression:=

**** The precedence flow in the descending order (high to low).

PEMDAS

PEMDAS helps us to remember the Python Operator Precedence Rule.

P – Parentheses

E – Exponent

M – Multiplication

D – Division

A – Addition

S – Subtraction

2.4.1. Example of Operator Precedence (Associativity)

According to the precedence order, the Multiplication, Division, Floor Division and Modulus see to have same level of precedence. To handle these peculiar situations, Python uses Associativity of the operators to evaluate the expression. The Associativity helps to choose the operator that should be computed first, i.e. the order of operations.

- **Associative Operators** – The associative operators such as multiplication, division, floor division and modulus except the exponent operator are executed from the *left* to the *right*.

- **Non- Associative Operators** – The comparison and Assignment operators does not involve with Associativity. The expressions with these operators are just evaluated from the *left* to the *right*.

```python
# program for Associativity
print("Assignment operators associativity")
x = 5*6/2//4%2
a = 2*4/2//6%5
print("The value of x: ",x)
print("The value of a: ",a)
y = 5%6//2/4*2
b = 2%4//2/6*5    # Execute from left to right
print("The value of y: ",y)
print("The value of b: ",b)
print("Non-Assignment operators associativity")
print("10>3<4: ",10>3<4)
print("10<3>4: ",10<3>4)
```

```
Assignment operators associativity
The value of x:  1.0
The value of a:  0.0
The value of y:  1.0
The value of b:  0.8333333333333333
Non-Assignment operators associativity
10>3<4:  True
10<3>4:  False
```

2.5. Changing Precedence and Associativity of Arithmetic Operators

To change the precedence and the associativity of the Arithmetic operators manually, the parentheses( ) are used.

```
# program using parentheses
a = 10+2*5
b = (10+2)*5
c = 10*2+5
d = 10*(2+5)
print(" By Operator Precedence: a = ",a)
print("By applying parentheses: b = ",b)
print(" By Operator Precedence: c = ",c)
print("By applying parentheses: d = ",d)

 By Operator Precedence: a =  20
By applying parentheses: b =  60
 By Operator Precedence: c =  25
By applying parentheses: d =  70
```

By applying parentheses, the operator precedence and associativity are changed manually thereby causing the change of results.

2.6. Translating Mathematical Formulae into Equivalent Python Expressions

The standard mathematical formulae or expression are not accepted in Python as it is and they have to be modified accordingly to the Python Script. For example; **(2 +4) (5) = 6 x 5** in Standard math but in Python, this expression might be consider as a callable function thereby stating an error. Therefore, the customary mathematical formulae are translated into their equivalent Python expressions.

Expressions	Standard Math	Python
(2+20)(3)	(2+20) x 3	(2+20)*3
$\dfrac{(3 + 10) + 5}{2}$	$\dfrac{(3 + 10) + 5}{2}$	(3+10)+5/2
$A = 4\pi r^2$	$A = 4\pi r^2$	A= 4*math.pi*r**2
$\sqrt{4}$	$\sqrt{4}$	math.sqrt(4)

Import Math Module

By importing the math module which is consisting of the math mathematical operations including.

- Mathematic constants
- Trigonometric functions
- Logarithmic functions
- Representations functions
- Angular functions

Some of the math () functions as the illustration.

1. *math.pi*

The mathematic constant of pie = 3.14 can be interpreted by the math.pie function.

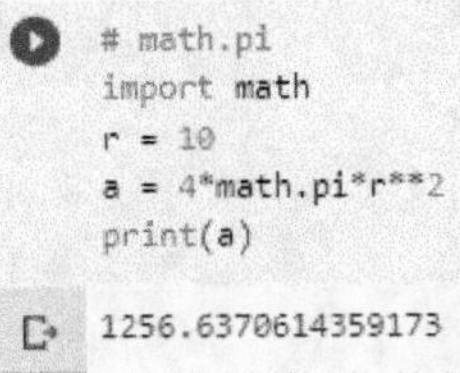

```python
# math.pi
import math
r = 10
a = 4*math.pi*r**2
print(a)
```

```
1256.6370614359173
```

2. *math.e*

The function returns the mathematical constant e =2.718.

```python
# math.e
import math
print("math.e = ",math.e)
a = 2* math.e
print("a = ",a)
```

```
math.e =   2.718281828459045
a =   5.436563656918099
```

3. *math.sin()*

The trigonometric value of Sine for the given value has been returned.

4. *math.cos()*

The trigonometric value of Cosine for the given value has been returned.

5. *math.tan()*

The trigonometric value of Tangent for the given value has been returned.

```python
# math.sin(),math.cos(), math.tan()
import math
a = 2
print("sin 2 = ", math.sin(a))
print("cos 2 = ", math.cos(a))
print("tan 2 = ", math.tan(a))
```

```
sin 2 =   0.9092974268256817
cos 2 =   -0.4161468365471424
tan 2 =   -2.185039863261519
```

6. *math.log()*

The logarithmic value of the given number will be calculated with eth base value of e and are returned by using this function.

```python
# math.log()
import math
print("log 4 = ",math.log(4))
print("log 8 = ",math.log(8))
```

```
log 4 =  1.3862943611198906
log 8 =  2.0794415416798357
```

7. *math.log10()*

The logarithmic value of base 10 has been obtained by this function.

```python
# math.log10()
import math
print("log 4 = ",math.log10(4))
print("log 8 = ",math.log10(8))
```

```
log 4 =  0.6020599913279624
log 8 =  0.9030899869919435
```

8. *math.sqrt()*

The function evaluates the square-root of the given number.

```python
# math.sqrt()
import math
x = 4
print("Square root of x = ",math.sqrt(x))
print("Square root of 90 = ",math.sqrt(90))
print("Square root of 27.9 = ",math.sqrt(27.9))
```

```
Square root of x =  2.0
Square root of 90 =  9.486832980505138
Square root of 27.9 =  5.282045058497703
```

9. *math.pow(x,y)*

The power of x for the consequent y has been returned.

```python
#math.pow(,)
import math
print ("Power of 2 by 3 = ",math.pow(2,3))
print ("Power of 34 by 6 = ",math.pow(34,6))
print("Power of 3 by -2 = ",math.pow(3,-2))
```

```
Power of 2 by 3 =  8.0
Power of 34 by 6 =  1544804416.0
Power of 3 by -2 =  0.1111111111111111
```

10. *math.floor()*

The greater or equal value of the given value has been returned as the floor value.

```python
#math.floor()
import math
print("floor value of 7.123 =", math.floor(7.123))
print("floor value of 16 =", math.floor(16))
print("floor value of-987.56 =", math.floor(-987.56))
```

```
floor value of 7.123 = 7
floor value of 16 = 16
floor value of-987.56 = -988
```

11. *math.fabs()*

The absolute value will be obtained from this function.

```python
# math.fabs()
import math
print("Absloute of 5.89 = ",math.fabs(5.89))
print("Absloute of -1 = ",math.fabs(-1))
print("Absloute of 9 = ",math.fabs(9))
```

```
Absloute of 5.89 =  5.89
Absloute of -1 =  1.0
Absloute of 9 =  9.0
```

12. *math.factorical()*

The factorial of the given integer value will be returned by the function.

```python
# math.factorial()
import math
print("Factorial part of 2 = ", math.factorial(2))
print("Factorial part of 16 = ", math.factorial(16))
```

```
Factorial part of 2 =  2
Factorial part of 16 =  20922789888000
```

13. math.modf()

The fractional partand integral of the number is evaluated by this function.

```python
# math.modf()
import math
print("Fractional and int of 34 = ",math.modf(34))
print("Fractional and int of 2.87 = ",math.modf(2.87))
print("Fractional and int of -6.076 = ",math.modf(-6.076))
```

```
Fractional and int of 34 =  (0.0, 34.0)
Fractional and int of 2.87 =  (0.8700000000000001, 2.0)
Fractional and int of -6.076 =  (-0.07599999999999962, -6.0)
```

14. math.inf

The function returns the infinity.

```python
# math. inf
import math
print("x = ",math.inf)
```

```
x =  inf
```

15. math.degreess()

The angular degrees are calculated by the function.

```python
# math.degrees
import math
print("Degrees of 4 = ", math.degrees(4))
print("Degrees of -5 = ", math.degrees(-5))
print("Degrees of 10 = ", math.degrees(10))
```

```
Degrees of 4 =   229.1831180523293
Degrees of -5 =   -286.4788975654116
Degrees of 10 =   572.9577951308232
```

2.7.   Bitwise Operator

Bitwise calculations on numeric integers are carried on by using the Bitwise Operators. The operations follow an atypical way by converting the given integer value into a binary value before implementing the bit-by-bit operation, hence has been termed as Bitwise operation. There are six Bitwise operators namely,

- Bitwise AND

- Bitwise OR

- Bitwise XOR

- Bitwise NOT

- Bitwise RIGHT shift

- Bitwise LEFT shift

2.7.1. The Bitwise AND (&) Operator

The integer value given has been converted into binary values and the bit-wise-bit operation has been carried out hence returning the 0s and 1s if the both of the bits have the same value of 0 or 1.

```
a = 10 (Decimal)
b= 6 (Decimal)
a & b = 1010 (Binary of 10)
        0110 (Binary of 6)
       ‾0010
a & b = 2 (Decimal for 0010)
```

```
# Bitwise AND Operator
a = 10
b = 6
print("Bitwise AND a&b: ", a&b)

Bitwise AND a&b:  2
```

2.7.2. The Bitwise OR (|) Operator

The integer value given has been converted into binary values and the bit-wise-bit operation has been carried out hence returning the value of 1 if either of the bits have 1, else 0.

```
a = 10 (Decimal)
b= 6 (Decimal)
a | b = 1010 (Binary of 10)
        0110 (Binary of 6)
        1110
a | b = 14 (Decimal for 1110)
```

```
# Bitwise OR Operator
a = 10
b = 6
print("Bitwise OR a|b: ", a|b)

Bitwise OR a|b:  14
```

2.7.3. The Bitwise XOR (^) Operator

The integer value given has been converted into binary values and the bit-wise-bit operation has been carried out hence returning the value of 1 only if either of the bits have 1, and 0 for same values.

a = 10 (Decimal)
b= 6 (Decimal)
a ^ b = 1010 (Binary of 10)
      0110 (Binary of 6)
      ‾‾‾‾‾‾
      1100
a ^ b = 12 (Decimal for 1100)
	▶ `# Bitwise XOR Operator`
	`a = 10`
	`b = 6`
	`print("Bitwise XOR a^b: ", a^b)`
	
	⤷ `Bitwise XOR a^b:   12`

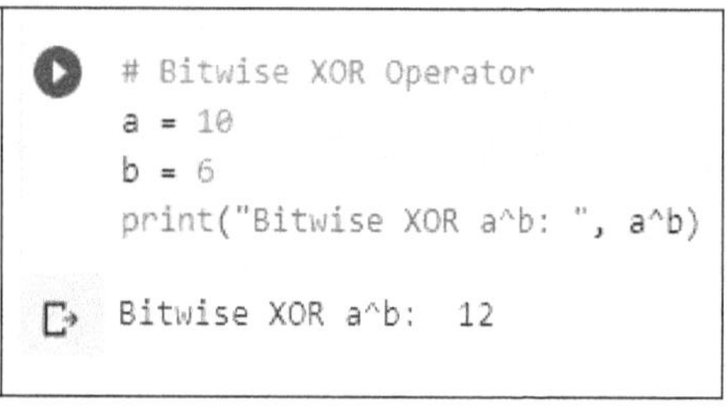

2.7.4. *The Right Shift (>>) Operator*

The shift occurs by moving the bits to the right and sealing the void space using the 0s. The shift is more like the consequence of dividing the given integer number by 2.

a = 10 (Decimal)
b= 6 (Decimal)
a = 1010 (Binary of 10)
| 0 | 1 | 0 | 1 | 0↓
a>>1= 0101 (Binary)
    = 5(Decimal)
b = 0110 (Binary of 6)
| 0 | 0 | 1 | 1 | 0↓
b>>1= 0011 (Binary)
    = 3(Decimal)
	▶ `# Bitwise RIGHT Shift Operator`
	`a = 10`
	`b = 6`
	`c =-10`
	`print("Bitwise RIGHT Shift a by 1: ", a>>1)`
	`print("Bitwise RIGHT Shift b by 1: ", b>>1)`
	`print("Bitwise RIGHT Shift c by 1:", c>>1)`
	
	⤷ `Bitwise RIGHT Shift a by 1:   5`
	`Bitwise RIGHT Shift b by 1:   3`
	`Bitwise RIGHT Shift c by 1: -5`

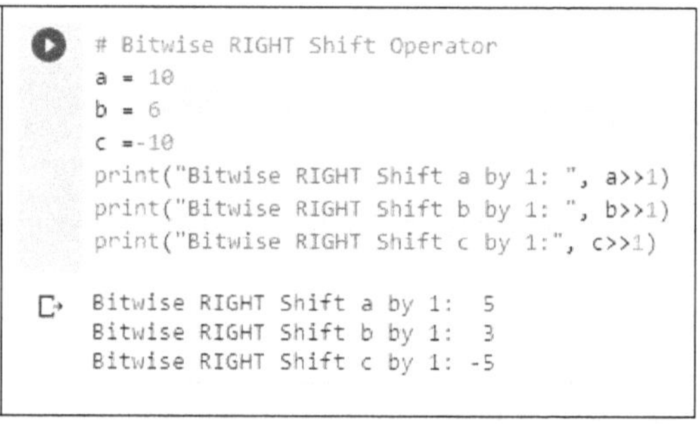

2.7.5. *The Left Shift (<<) Operator*

The shift occurs by moving the bits to the left and sealing the void space using the 0s. The shift is more like the consequence of multiplying the given integer number by 2 or some power of 2.

a = 10 (Decimal)
b= 6 (Decimal)
a = 1010 (Binary of 10)
| 0 | 0 | 0 | 1 | | 0 | 1 | 0 | 0 |
a<<1= 0001 0100 (Binary)
    = 20(Decimal)
b = 0110 (Binary of 6)
| 0 | 0 | 0 | 0 | | 1 | 1 | 0 | 0 |
b<<1= 0000 1100 (Binary)
    = 12(Decimal)
	▶ `# Bitwise LEFT Shift Operator`
	`a = 10`
	`b = 6`
	`c =-10`
	`print("Bitwise LEFT Shift a by 1: ", a<<1)`
	`print("Bitwise LEFT Shift b by 1: ", b<<1)`
	`print("Bitwise LEFT Shift c by 1:", c<<1)`
	
	⤷ `Bitwise LEFT Shift a by 1:   20`
	`Bitwise LEFT Shift b by 1:   12`
	`Bitwise LEFT Shift c by 1: -20`

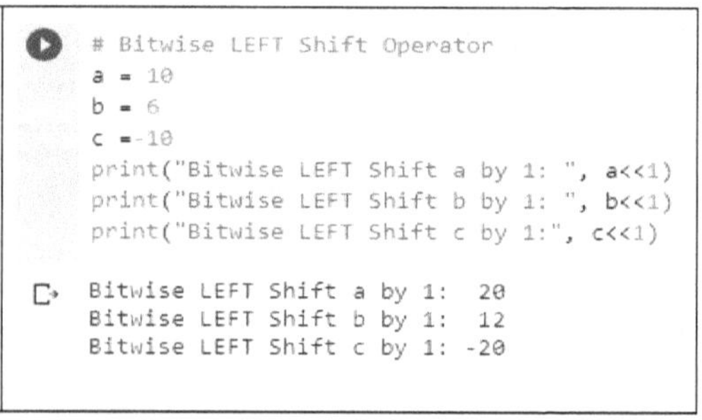

2.8. The Compound Assignment Operator

The compound Assignment operator is combine form two different operations. The rear operation has been executed based on the consequence of the forefront operation. Consider '+=' operator, a comb of addition and assignment operations. The + operator first performs the addition process and the = operator assigns that solution as the result.

The compound assignment operations are:

Arithmetic and Assignment	Bitwise and Assignment
• += - Addition Assignment	• &= -Bitwise AND Assignment
• -+ - Subtraction Assignment	• |= - Bitwise OR Assignment
• *= - Multiplication Assignment	• ^= - Bitwise XOR Assignment
• /= - Division Assignment	• <<= - Bitwise LEFT Assignment
• //= - Floor Division Assignment	• >>= - Bitwise RIGHT Assignment
• %= - Modulus Assignment	
• **= - Exponent Assignment	

```python
# Compound Assignmet for Arithmetic Operators
a = 2
print("a =",a)
a += 4
print("Addition and Assignment of a += 4 : ",a)
a -= 2
print("\nSubtraction and Assignment of a -= 2 : ", a)
a *= 5
print("\nMultiplication and Assignment of a *= 5 : ", a)
a /= 2
print("\nDivision and Assignment of a /= 2 : ", a)
a %= 5
print("\nModulus and Assignment of a %= 5 :" ,a)
a //= 2
print("\nFloor Divison and Assignment of a //= 2 :", a)
a **= 3
print("\nExponent and Assignment of a **= 3 :", a)
```

```
a = 2
Addition and Assignment of a += 4 :   6

Subtraction and Assignment of a -= 2 :   4

Multiplication and Assignment of a *= 5 :   20

Division and Assignment of a /= 2 :   10.0

Modulus and Assignment of a %= 5 : 0.0

Floor Divison and Assignment of a //= 2 : 0.0

Exponent and Assignment of a **= 3 : 0.0
```

```python
# Compound Assignmet for Bitwise Operators
a =2
print("a=",a)
a &= 2
print("Bitwise AND and Assignment of a &= 2 : ",a)
a |= 1
print("\nBitwise OR and Assignment of a |= 1 : ", a)
a ^= 5
print("\nBitwise XOR and Assignment of a ^= 5 : ", a)
a <<= 2
print("\nBitwise LEFT SHIFT and Assignment of a <<= 2 : ", a)
a >>= 1
print("\nBitwise RIGHT SHIFT and Assignment of a >>= 1 :" ,a)
```

```
a= 2
Bitwise AND and Assignment of a &= 2 :  2

Bitwise OR and Assignment of a |= 1 :  3

Bitwise XOR and Assignment of a ^= 5 :  6

Bitwise LEFT SHIFT and Assignment of a <<= 2 :  24

Bitwise RIGHT SHIFT and Assignment of a >>= 1 : 12
```

Summary

This chapter gives an introduction to Python Operators and Expression. You learned about different types of operators and how to use them with simple programs. Also you know how to translate Mathematical Formulae into Equivalent Python Expressions.

References

Web

- docs.python.org
- techvidvan.com
- programiz.com
- mathcs. emory.edu
- journaldev.com

Book

- Python Programming - Python Programming for Beginners, Adam Stewart, 2016.

2.9.   Test Your Skill

Multiple Choice Questions

1.   Which statement is used to combine various arithmetic operators?

   a)   Augmented Assignment Statement

   b)   Simple Assignment Statement

   c)   Add Assignment Statement

   d)   Multi-line Statement

2.   Which operator takes a single operand to perform an operation?

   a)   Binary Operator

   b)   Unary Operator

   c)   Ternary Operator

   d)   Single Operator

3.   Which operators yield the highest priority of execution?

   a)   Lowest Precedence Operators

   b)   High-level Operators

   c)   Highest Precedence Operators

   d)   Precedence Operators

4.   Which of the following is the lowest precedence operator?

   a)   ()

   b)   []

   c)   <

   d)   <<

5.   The associative operators such as multiplication, division, floor division and modulus except the exponent operator are executed from ___________

   a)   Right to Left

   b)   Left to Right

   c)   Center

   d)   None of the mentioned

6.   To change the precedence and the associativity of the arithmetic operators manually, ___________ are used.

   a)   Braces {}

   b)   Brackets []

   c)   Parentheses ( )

   d)   Unary Operators +,-

7. The mathematic constant of pie (3.14) can be interpreted by ____________ function.

   a) math.pi

   b) math.pi[]

   c) math.pie[]

   d) math.pie

8. Which function can be used to obtain the absolute value?

   a) math.fabs()

   b) math.fabs[]

   c) math.fab

   d) math.fab()

9. Which of the following is not a bitwise operator?

   a) Bitwise NOT

   b) Bitwise RIGHT shift

   c) Bitwise LEFT shift

   d) Bitwise MIDDLE shift

10. Which of the following is a compound assignment operator?

   a) <

   b) >

   c) <<

   d) ^=

Review Questions

1. What are Multi line statements?
2. What is the purpose of // operator?
3. What is the purpose of is operator?
4. Explain the various types of operators in Python.
5. List out the operator precedence in Python.

CHAPTER 3

3. Decision Statements

Learning Outcomes

- Describe the usage of Boolean operators and its type.
- Perform operations on numbers and Strings with Boolean operators.
- Perform operations using Boolean expressions and relational operators.
- Describe the working of simple decision-making statements and its implementations with if statement, if-else statement and its implementations, nested if and its implementations and multi way if-elif-else statements.
- Explain the conditional expression and its uses for writing programs.

Importance of Decision Statements

- Decisions in program is used when a program has conditional has conditional choices to execute a code block.
- It is a logical decision, provides decision making statements to make prompt decision for an application based on the user requirement.

3.1.   Introduction

Control structure governs the execution of the program. **Programmer can decide which statement should be executed based on the condition. Boolean expression is similar to control structure with a condition.**

In this chapter we will discuss briefly about the Boolean operators. Boolean expression is a logical expression which evaluates one of two states whether true or false. Python gives a Boolean type that can be either true or false. When you compare two values the expression returns a Boolean answer.

3.2.   Boolean Type

Python has a data type named as **'bool'**. It evaluates the condition whether a condition is either True or False. It has two values 1(True) or 0 (False) It was first introduced by George Boole in 1854 The term bool was driven by the name of the George Boole. bool () function will allow you to evaluate the type of two value belong to that type 'bool'.

3.3. Boolean Operators

Logical operators such as and, or and not are referred as Boolean operators. There are three operators.

S. No	Operator	Function
1.	And	+
2.	OR	*
3.	NOT	^

3.3.1. And Operator

And operator needs two operands and operator, performs logical AND of the two operators.

Operator	Meaning	Example
And	True if both are true	A and B

Truth Table

X	And	Y	Returns
True	And	True	True
True	And	False	False
False	And	True	False
False	And	False	False

```
[1]  True and True
 ⊡  True

 ▶  True and False
 ⊡  False

[2]  False and True
 ⊡  False

[3]  False and False
 ⊡  False
```

3.3.2. OR Operator

OR operator needs two operands and one operator, it performs logical OR of the two operators.

Operator	Meaning	Example
OR	True if at least one is True	A OR B

Truth Table

X	And	Y	Returns
True	OR	True	True
True	OR	False	True
False	OR	True	True
False	OR	False	False

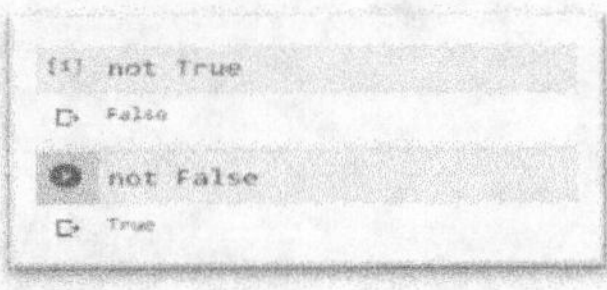

3.3.3. NOT Operator

NOT operator needs one operand and one operator, performs logical NOT of the operator.

Operator	Meaning	Example
NOT	True if it is FALSE	Not A

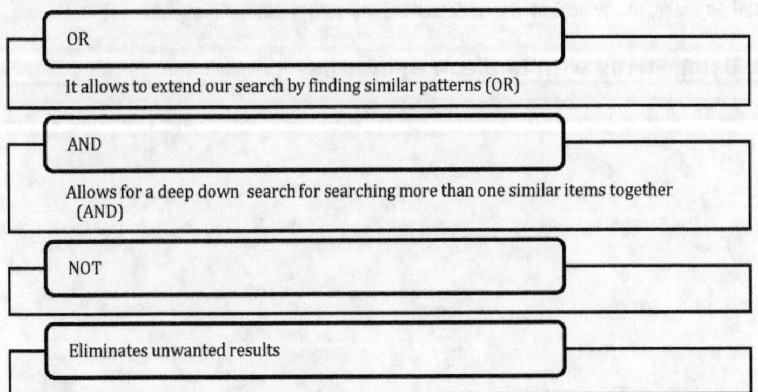

Advantages of Boolean Operator

OR

It allows to extend our search by finding similar patterns (OR)

AND

Allows for a deep down search for searching more than one similar items together (AND)

NOT

Eliminates unwanted results

Disadvantages of Boolean Operator

- It is difficult to translate a query into a expression.

Applications of Boolean Operator

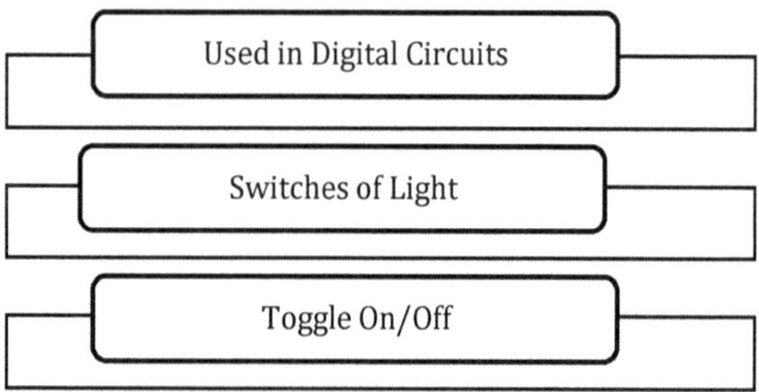

3.4. Using Numbers with Boolean Operators

A python Program allow numbers with Boolean operator, here we illustrated some examples.

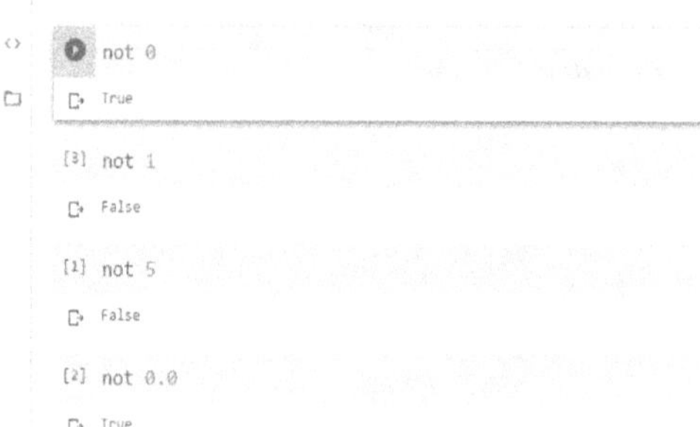

From above example, we use not operator on the numbers and all numbers are true. 0(Zero) is treated as False, likewise 5 is also treated as true so not of 5 is false.

3.5. Using String with Boolean Operators

Python program can use string as Boolean operators. Empty string is always evaluated as True.

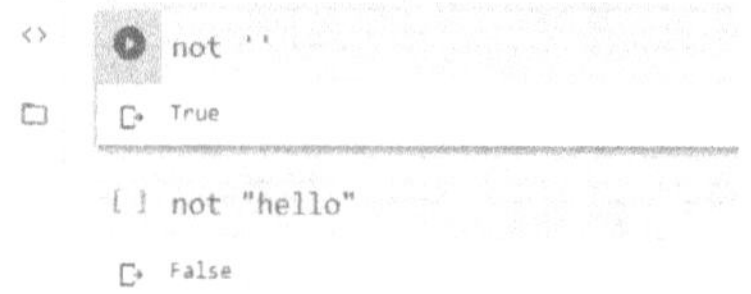

3.6. Using Relational Operators

Relational operators are used for establishing a relationship between the two operands. operators are less than<, Greater than > and Equal To =. Python is capable to understand the relational operator and return the logical values whether True or False.

It compares two values and produce results. The following example shows how Boolean Expression are used in relational operators.

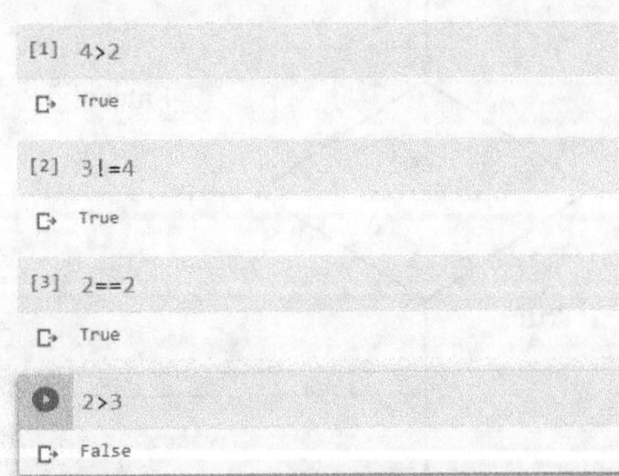

Operator	Meaning	Example	Return Value
>	Greater than	4>2	True
<	Less than	2<3	True
>=	Greater than or equal to	4>=4	True
<=	Less than or equal to	4<=3	True
!=	Not equal to	3! =4	True

3.7. Decision Making Statements

Python supports various decision-making statements.

- If statements
- If -else statements
- Nested If statements
- Multi way if-elif-else statements.

We will discuss each of them in detail.

3.7.1. if Statements

If statement will execute when a given condition is true.

The Syntax of if Statement is

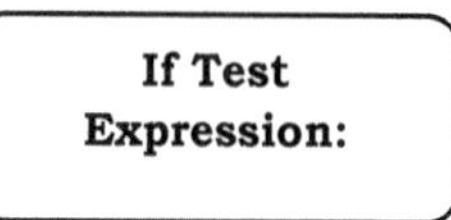

Flow Chart

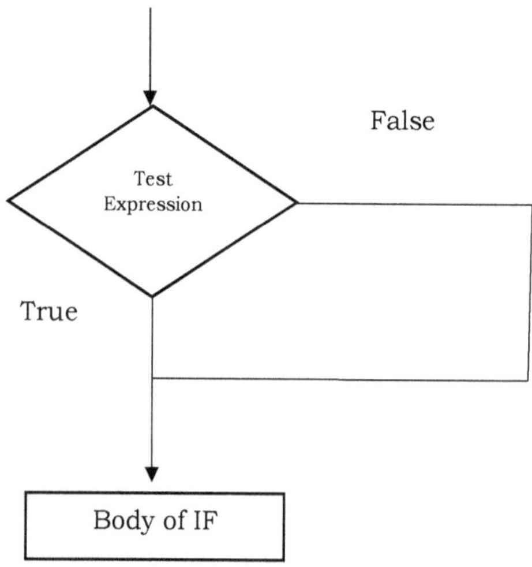

Explanation

The body of the if Statement indicates by an indentation. If the statement is true the following block of statement will be executed and if the condition returns to false the control of the loop will be terminated.

Example 1

```python
age = int(input("Enter the Age : "));
if age >= 18:
    print("\n Eligible to Vote ")
```

```
Enter the Age : 34

    Eligible to Vote
```

The above example checks whether a person is eligible to get a driving license or not. The condition is if person age is above and equal to 18, he is eligible to get a driving license.

```
days=int(input("\n Enter the days in the Month\n"));

if days==31:
  print("\nGood, You are right\n ")
```

```
enter the days in the month
31

Good, You are right
```

Example 2

Applications of if Statement in Real World Scenario

Weather Monitoring System

It will find by analysing the weather if the weather is cloudy it will alert the user to take umbrella.

```
If (climate==cloud)
{
Alert" Take Umbrella";
}
```

Advantages	Disadvantages
when a condition is true and execute a set of block codes.	If the condition fails it exits from the loop
Executes in a easier way	There is no optional statements

3.7.2. The if-else Statement

If else statement evaluates condition if the condition is true, the body of the if part will be executed. If the condition is false the else part will be executed.

The SYNTAX of the Statement is

```
If test expression:
     Body of if
     Else:
     Body of Else
```

Flow Chart

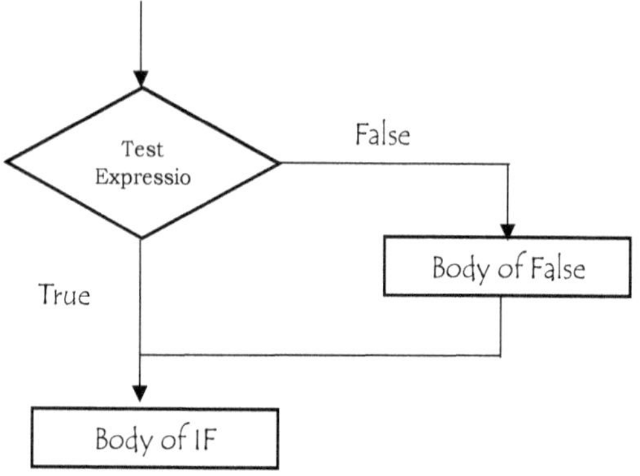

Example of If Else

```
i=int(input("\n Enter the Number"));
if (i>=18):
  print("\n Eligible to Vote")
else:
  print("\n Not Eligible to Vote")
```

```
Enter the Age17

Not Eligible to Vote
```

Explanation

The above example validates whether a person is eligible to vote or not. The condition is if person age is above or equal to 18, he is eligible to vote, or if the person is below 18 the above condition is false the following false block will be executed.

Example

```
a=int(input("\nEnter a Number\n"))
b=int(input("\nEnter a Number\n"))
if b>a:
    print("b is greater than a")
else:
    print("a is greater than b")
```

```
Enter a Number
34

Enter a Number
56
b is greater than a
```

Explanation

The above example checks whether a number is greater than the other. The condition is if number 1 is greater than number 2, if block will be executed. if the above condition is false the false block will be executed.

Real Time Example

- Plant watering system

If the plant is dry, it alerts the gardener to water the plant else it alerts the gardener water that plant is wet.

```
If (moist<=100)
{
Alert "Do not water the plant"
}
Else
{
Alert "Water it"
}
```

Usage

- Easy monitoring
- Sufficient watering is encouraged.

Advantages and Disadvantages

Advantages	Disadvantages
- Overcomes the disadvantages of If statement	- If indentation is not specified it is difficult for the programmer.
- It is works great for variable conditions.	- Speed of the program depends on the number of conditions

3.7.3. The nested if Statements

Any number of if statement can be nested one and another that is called nested if statement. There may certain situations where we evaluate true can check for another condition.

The Syntax is

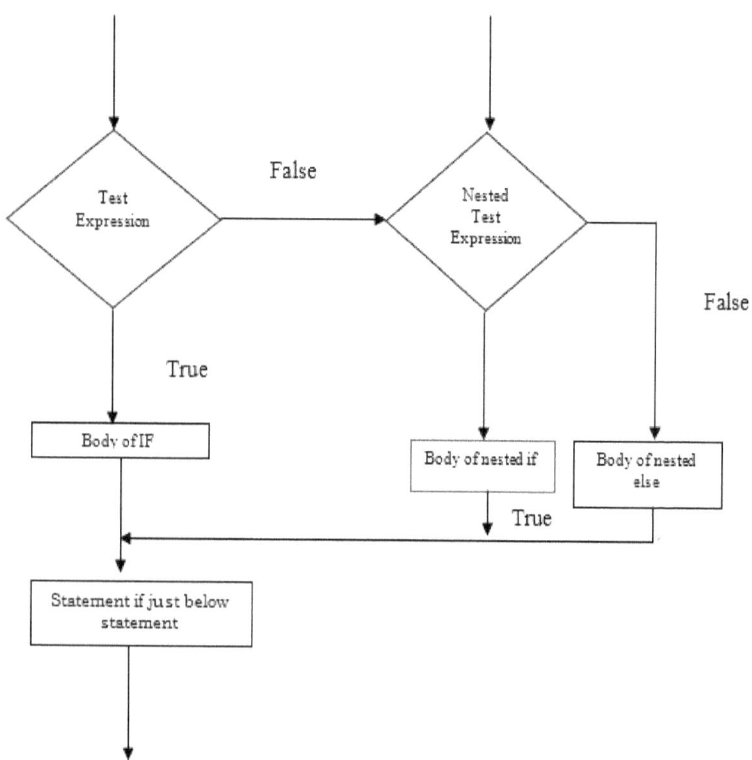

Flow Chart

Example 1

```
x=int(input("Enter Your Age"))
if x>21:
  if x>100:
    print("You are too old")
  else:
      print("Welcome!,You are at the right age")
else:
      print("you are too young")
```

```
Enter Your Age34
Welcome!,You are at the right age
```

Explanation

The above program is programmed to find the age of graduation in college. If the student is above 100 years, he/she is not eligible.

Example 2

```
itemsOrdered =int(input("\nenter the item\n"));
itemsInStock = 32;

print("Got an order for", itemsOrdered, "items. In stock:", itemsInStock)
# Compare order size against inventory
if itemsOrdered >= itemsInStock:
    print("Resupply the inventory. We're running out!")
else:
    packageCount = round(itemsOrdered / 8)

    if packageCount > 1:
      print("We need multiple packages to fulfil this order!")
```

```
enter the item
67
Got an order for 67 items. In stock: 32
Resupply the inventory. We're running out!
```

Explanation

The above program is programmed to find the stock retain in the retail store. If the stock is above than the ordered item will request the user to wait until the stock is back.

Real Time Application

- **Voting System**

The first condition is the person should be above 18 years and he/she should have voter id card for voting. Only if both the conditions ae true the person can vote in election or he/she cannot vote.

If(age>=18)

{

If (voter id==yes)

{

Allowed the person vote

}

Else {

Apply for voter ID.

}

Else

{

Not Eligible

}

Advantages and Disadvantages

Advantages	Disadvantages
• No limitations	• Too much of nesting can cause confusion
• Efficiently used for complex programs	• Higher the complexity higher the difficulty.

3.7.4. Multi-way if-elif-else Statements

The elif in short termed as else if. It is used to check for multiple expressions in various applications.

- It checks for the condition for if, if the condition is False, it checks the condition for the next elif block and so on.

- If all the conditions are False, body of else will be executed.

- Only one block among the several if...elif...else blocks is executed according to the condition.

- The if block can have only one else block. But it can have multiple elif blocks.

Syntax

```
If test expression:
Body of if elif test
expression
Body of elif
```

Flowchart

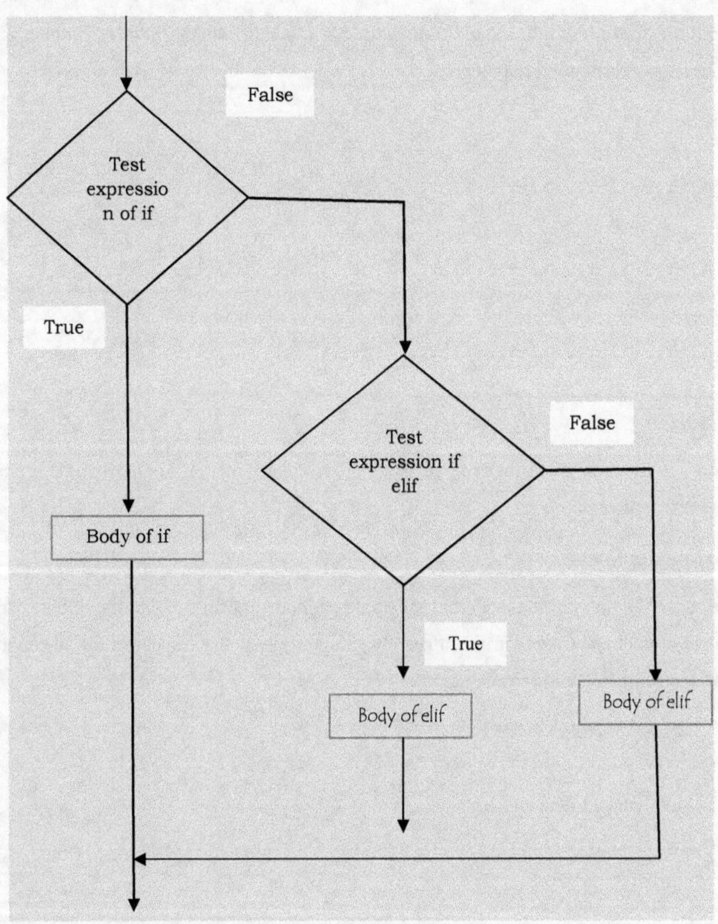

Example

```
num=int(input("\tEnter the number\t"));
if 9 < num < 99:
  print("Two digit number")
elif 99 < num < 999:
    print("Three digit number")
elif 999 < num < 9999:
      print("Four digit number")
else:
        print("number is <= 9 or >= 9999")


        Enter the number       12
Two digit number
```

Explanation

From the above example, the program is used to calculate whether a given number is two-digit number or three-digit number.

Example

```
num=int(input("\nenter the Number\n"));
if num > 0:
    print("Positive number")
elif num == 0: print("Zero")
else:
    print("Negative number")
```

```
enter the Number
-9
Negative number
```

Explanation

From the above example, the program is used to calculate whether a given number is positive number or negative number.

Real Time Application

Electricity bill generation is a real time application for multiple if else statements because the calculation of electricity varies differently. So multiple if else calculates for all conditions and produces the following result.

```
If (cuint>=100)
{
Elec= cunit*150+100
}
Elif(cuint>=200)
{
Elec= cunit*250+200
}
Else
{
Print("Free for 100 units spent")
}
```

Advantages and Disadvantages

Advantages	Disadvantages
• For Situations involving series of decisions multi way if else is used efficiently.	• Too much of decision can cause complexity
• Efficiently handles all data types	• Hard to learn.

3.8.   Conditional Expressions

Conditional expressions is also called as ternary operator. This evaluates a set of statements based on the condition whether true or false. It is so compact than multiway if else statement. A single line of code can execute the test condition.

$$\boxed{\textbf{[On\_true] if [expression]}\\ \textbf{else [on\_false]}}$$

Example 1

```
a=int(input("\nEnter a number \n" ));
b=int(input("\nEnter a number \n" ));
c= a if a > b else b
print("Largest number is",c)

Enter a number
50

Enter a number
60
Largest number is 60
```

Explanation

Gets two numbers from the user. Evaluates a test condition whether a is greater than b if a is greater will print or it will print b.

Example 2

```
n = int(input("Enter  the number:"))
print("The Number is Divisible by Four") if n % 4 == 0 else print("The Number is not Divisible by Four");

Enter  the number:23
The Number is not Divisible by Four
```

Explanation

The above program is programmed to calculate whether a given number is divisible by four or not. If the particular number is divisible by four, the condition is true, the if statement will be executed. If the condition is false the else part will be executed.

Real Time Application

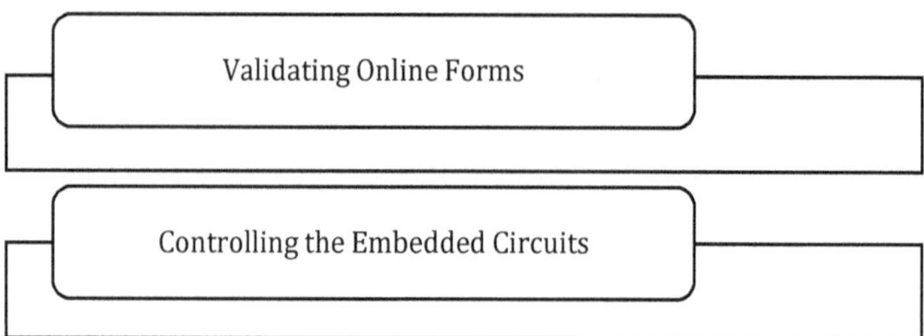

Advantages and Disadvantages

Advantages	Disadvantages
• Optimum line of code	• Compiler treats ternary operator differently it effects in efficient of the program
• Easy debugging	• It is not readable

Summary

Decision making is anticipation of condition occurring while execution of the program and specifying actions taken according to the conditions. An if statement can be followed by an optional else statement, which executes Boolean expression is false. And, Or, not operations are in Boolean operators. Numbers, Strings, Relational operators are also used.

References

[1]   geeksforgeeks.org/control-structures-in-programming-languages

[2]   https://problemsolvingwithpython.com/04-Data-Types-and-Variables/04.02-Boolean-Data-Type/#:~:text=The%20boolean%20data%20type%20is,the%20True%20and%20False%20keywords.&text=The%20output%20%3Cclass%20'bool',is%20a%20boolean%20data%20type.

[3]   https://beginnersbook.com/2018/01/python-if-elif-else/#:~:text=There%20can%20be%20multiple%20'elif,is%20evaluated%20and%20so%20on.

[4]   https://www.google.com/search?q=if+elif+else+in+python&rlz=1C1CHBF_enIN864IN864&sxsrf=ALeKk01zFQqj7piXjpY5ZYj5XM21tnrPyA:1597387901662&source=lnms&tbm=isch&sa=X&ved=2ahUKEwiwucnTjZrrAhX3yzgGHfkxAmUQ_AUoAXoECA4QAw&biw=1517&bih=730#imgrc=BW08t1C4i9jjuM

3.9.   Test Your Skill

Choose the Right Answer

1. Python has a data type named as ____________

    a) Tool

    b) bool

    c) int

    d) variable

2. ____________ Such as and, or and not are referred as Boolean operators.

    a) Numerical operations

    b) mathematical operations

    c) logical operations

    d) sign values

3. ____________ Operator needs two operands and operator.

    a)   And

    b) or

    c) else

    d) not

4. Any number of if statement can be nested one and another that is called ________ statement.

    a) If else

    b) nested else if

    c) else if

    d) nested if

5. ____________ Operators are used for establishing a relationship between the two operands.

    a) Logical

    b) numerical

    c) arithmetic

    d) relational

6. If statement will execute when a given condition is ____________

    a) Either true or false

    b) true

    c) false

    d) none

7. Empty string is always evaluated as ____________

   a) Empty

   b) true

   c) false

   d) zero

8. Conditional expressions is also called as ____________ operator.

   a) Bit-wise

   b) multiple

   c) ternary

   d) end

9. ____________ governs the execution of the program.

   a) Control structure

   b) conditions

   c) data

   d) loop structure

10. Electricity bill generation is a real time application for ____________ statements.

   a) If else

   b) if

   c) switch

   d) multiple if else

Answer the Following Briefly

1. Enumerate Boolean operators.

2. Discuss about relational operators?

3. Define Decision making statements.

4. State if-else statement with one example.

5. List the applications of if statement in Real world scenario.

CHAPTER 4

4. Loop Control Statements

Learning Outcomes

- Describe the working of while loop and its implementations with some of the examples.
- Describe the working of for loop and its implementations with some of the examples.
- Explain the working of nested loop and its implementations with some of the examples.
- Describe the working of control and break statement and its implementations with some of the examples.

Importance of Loops

- Loops are important in any programming language as it helps to execute a block of code repeatedly.
- In some cases, we need to use a block code over and over, but it is not possible to write many times. At this time loops are used.
- The looping simplifies the complex problems into easier.

4.1. Introduction

Control statement is needed to control the flow of execution of the program. Loop control statements is a programming structure will execute a block of statements multiple times until a particular condition, Unlike Control flow it just control the execution of the program but loop control statement will allow the program structure to execute continuously. in real world applications, For example, the programmer wants to display all numbers less than 1000, in that case it is difficult for the programmer to do that manually, so it is advisable to go for loop control statements. Break and continue statements are also used for terminating and continuing the program from execution.

In this chapter will discuss briefly about loop control statements like for, while and nested for loop and its execution with some examples. Will also describe the working of break, continue and pass statement with examples.

Advantages of Loops

1. It provides code re-usability.
2. Using loops, it is not necessary to write the same code repeatedly.
3. Using loops, traversal of elements over data structures (arrays or linked list) are possible.

4.2. The While Loop

In while loop, programmer can iterate a particular block of code repeatedly until the test expression is true. Programmer can use while loop when he/she do not know how many times to iterate. When the program control reaches the while loop, the condition is checked. If the condition is true, the body of while is executed.

4.2.1. Details of the While Loop

Syntax

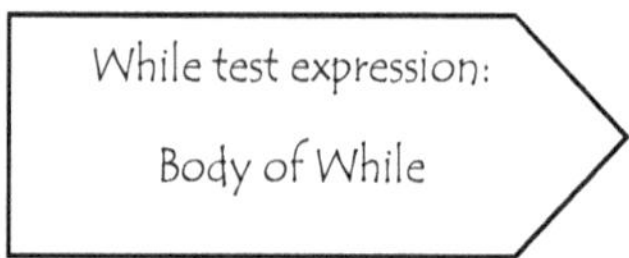

In while loop,

- Check for the test expression.
- If it is true the block of code in while will be execute once.
- Control will check for the test expression again if it is true, it will execute the block of code.
- Step 3 is repeated until the test expression is evaluate false.

Else Statement for While Loop

A while loop may have an optional else block. The else part is executed if the condition in the while loop evaluates false. The while loop can terminated with a break statement. At this case else statement can be ignored.

Example

```
counter = 2
while counter < 3:
    print("Inside loop")
    counter = counter + 1
else:
    print("Inside else")
```

```
Inside loop
Inside loop
Inside loop
Inside else
```

Explanation

The counter variable is used to print the string inside loop three times. It executes till it prints third time. In the fourth iteration, the condition of while becomes false, the else is executed.

4.2.2. *Flowchart of While Loop*

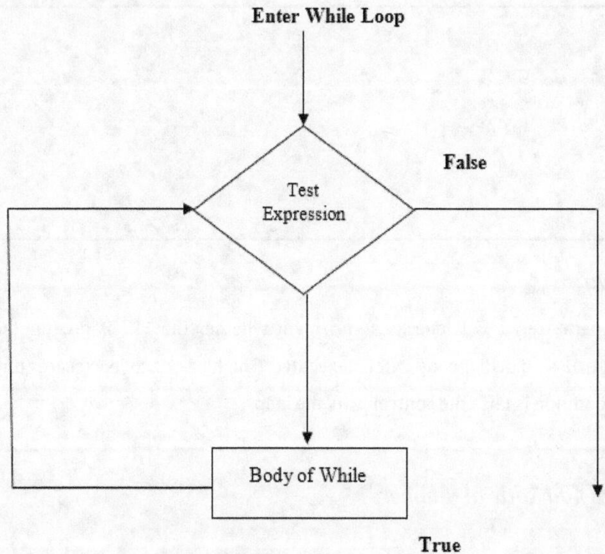

Figure 1: Operation of While Loop

4.2.3. *Examples on While*

Example 1

```
num=0;
while(num<5):
  num=num+1
  print('The Count is:',num)

The Count is: 1
The Count is: 2
The Count is: 3
The Count is: 4
The Count is: 5
```

Explanation

Assigns the num =0 for avoiding memory dumping in the variable. It checks the statement whether the num is less than 5. Yes zero is less than five so the condition is true, now the variable num is incremented by 1. The block of code executes until it reaches 5. If the condition is false the control exits the loop.

Example 2

```
temperature = 115
while temperature > 112:
    temperature = temperature - 1
    print('temperature is',temperature)


temperature is 114
temperature is 113
temperature is 112
```

Explanation

The temperature =115 It checks a statement whether the 112 is greater than 115. The condition is true so block of code will be executed. The block of code executes until it reaches 115. if the condition is false the control exits the loop.

Example 3

Program to Add Natural Numbers

```
n = 5
sum = 0
i = 1
while i <= n:
    sum = sum + i
    i = i+1
print("The sum is",sum)


The sum is 15
```

Explanation

The n (natural numbers) = 5 It checks the statement whether i is less than or equal to n. The condition is true and the iteration is repeated until it reaches 5 and display 15 by adding the natural numbers from 1 to 5. If is the false the control exists the loop.

Applications

Consulting the doctor is the best example for while loop. We will consult the doctor until we are cured completely i.e. until all our positive results should change to negative result, likewise the loop will executes repeatedly until the condition becomes false.

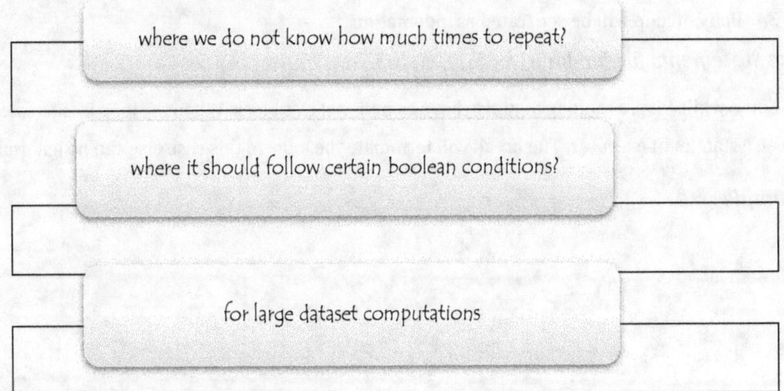

Advantages and Disadvantages

Advantages	Disadvantages
Executes the code repeatedly until it accomplishes the goal	It checks the condition for each iteration
Easy understanding	It is slow for large computations
Easy execution	Code is not readable

4.3. For Loop

For loop repeats the control structure to efficient. Writes a loop which has to execute for a specified sequence such as list or strings.

4.3.1. Details of for Loop

It has Two Parts

- Header
- Body

Header part specifies the declarations of the variable and body part specifies the execution of block of code when the condition is true.

Syntax

```
For val in sequence:
    Body of For
```

1. Val variable that takes value from the item inside the sequence on each iteration.
2. Loop will be executed until we reach the last item in the sequence.
3. Body of loop will be separated as indentation.

Else Statements for for-loop

Like a while loop, a for loop may also have an optional else block. When the loop is exhausted, the else statement executes. The break will terminate the loop, in this case else can be ignored.

Example

```
digits = [0,1,5]
for i in digits:
    print(i)
else:
    print("No items left")


0
1
5
No items left
```

Explanation

Initialize the digits with three elements. The digits are prints until the loop reaches the third element. When the third element is reached, the else block is executed and prints "no elements left".

Flowchart

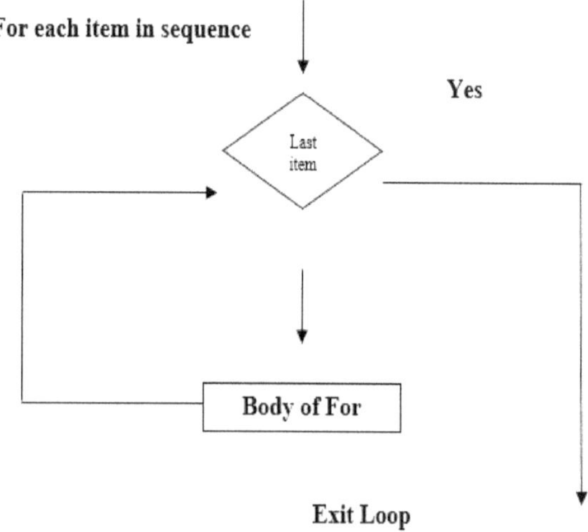

4.3.2. Some More Programs on for Loop

Calculate the Sum of Values in List Using for Loop

Example 1

```
numbers = [10, 15, 3, 8, 4, 2, 5, 4, 11]

# variable to store the sum
sum = 0

# iterate over the list
for val in numbers:
  sum = sum+val

print("The sum is", sum)
```

```
The sum is 62
```

Explanation

Initialize the list with 10 numbers. Sum is initialized to zero at the beginning now Calculate the sum of numbers in the list, adding all numbers using for loop. For each number list is added and stored in sum. Sum variable is now displayed.

Example 2

```
numbers = ['one', 'two', 'three']
for number in numbers:
    print('Current number:', number)

print("Good bye!")
```

```
Current number: one
Current number: two
Current number: three
Good bye!
```

Explanation

Initializing the list with three elements, using for loop variable checks for each sequence of iteration and prints the current number which is stored in number variable. When the sequence of iteration completes the control will be exited from the loop.

Real Time Example

Travelling in a bus that goes around and around until there are passengers in the bus. When there are no passengers, the bus immediately stops from travelling the city. likewise, for loop executes until the set of sequence is available.

Situations to Handle for Loop

- When we iterate through array or list or strings.
- When set of statements has to run for definite number of times.
- For large dataset computation.

Advantages and Disadvantages

Advantages	Disadvantages
• Possibility of error is eliminated	• It cannot travel in a reverse fashion
• Code can be readable	• Can't skip the elements
• No use of indexing in this loop	• There should be proper indention

4.4. Nested Loops

Loops can be nested as one loop into another loop. Nested loop is a loop which is blended with one or more loops. Similar to nested if statements.

Syntax

```
for [first iterating variable] in [outer loop]:

    [statement(s)]

for [second iterating variable] in [nested loop]:

    [statement (s)]
```

- Program executes the outer loop first.
- First iteration triggers inner loop and execute its statement.
- After the inner loop completes it triggers the outer loop statement.
- Repeats the step until the loops gets terminated by itself.

Flow Chart

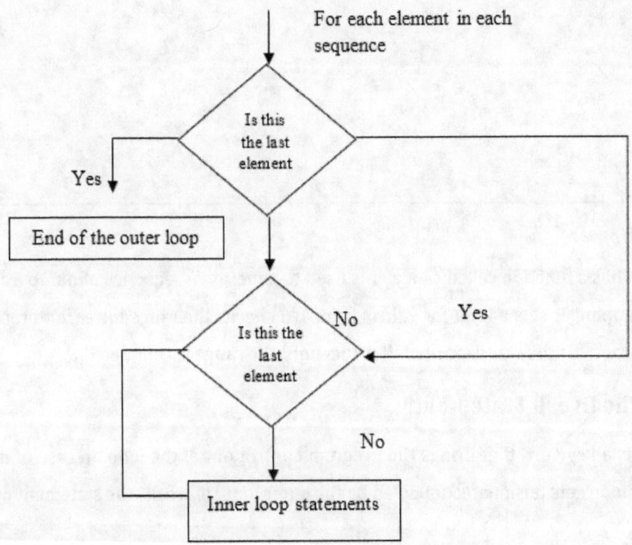

4.4.1. Some More Programs on Nested Loops

Example 1

```python
num_list = [1,2,3]
alpha_list = ['a', 'b', 'c']

for number in num_list:
    print(number)
    for letter in alpha_list:
        print(letter)
```

```
1
a
b
c
2
a
b
c
3
a
b
c
```

Explanation

First statement executes the inner loop and print the number 1, then the control executes outer loop and print the alphabet a, this iterates up to the end of the element in the sequence.

Example 2

```python
for i in range(1,6):
    for j in range(i):
        print("*",end=' ')
    print()
```
```
*
* *
* * *
* * * *
* * * * *
```

Explanation

Python has a function called range. It is used to generate a sequence of numbers range () is used for looping. It sets a limit for values from 1-6 checks the range for each iteration of i. for every iteration of i the star is printed. It prints until the range is completed.

4.5.   The Break Statement

Break is a keyword that brings the program control out of the loop. In case of nested loop first inner loop gets terminated followed by the outer loop. It breaks the statement one by one.

Syntax

Flowchart

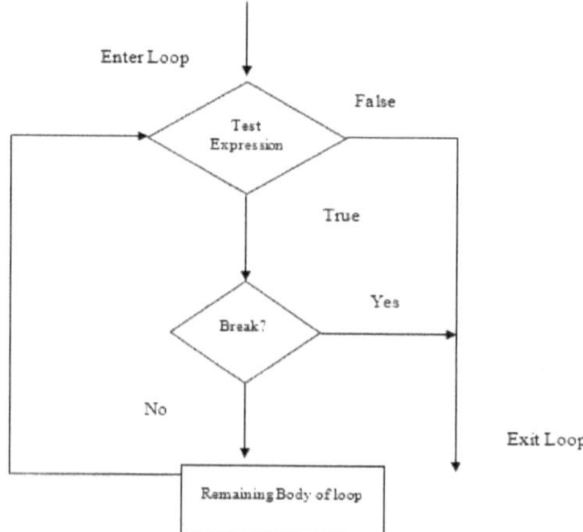

Example 1

```
for i in range(5):
    if i > 3:
        break
    print(i)

0
1
2
3
```

Explanation

It checks for certain condition when the condition is true, it immediately terminates from the program. When i is greater than 5 it terminates from the loop.

Example 2

```
for val in "string":
    if val == "i":
        break
    print(val)

s
t
r
```

Explanation

It checks for certain condition when the condition is true, it immediately terminates from the program. When val value is equal to i it terminates from the loop.

4.6.   The Continue Statement

Continue is a **keyword** used in python. The **continue** statement in Python will return the control to the beginning of the loop. It will reject all the remaining statements in the current iteration of the loop and moves the control back to the top of the loop. It is used in both for and while loop.

Syntax

#Loop Statements
Continue;

Flowchart

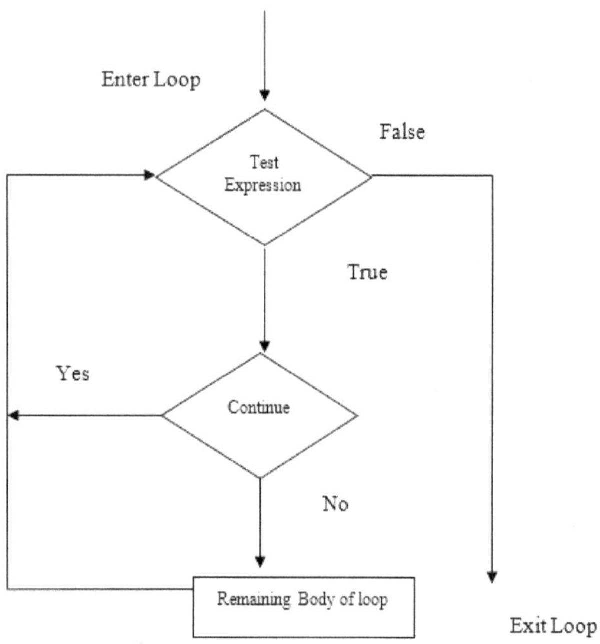

Example 1

```python
for letter in 'Python':
    if letter == 'h':
        continue
    print('Current Letter :', letter)

Current Letter : P
Current Letter : y
Current Letter : t
Current Letter : o
Current Letter : n
```

Explanation

It checks for certain condition when the condition is true, it executes the program. When control comes to continue statement, exits the loop and comes back again to loop. When the letter is equal to h it terminates from the loop and executes the remaining part.

Example 2

```
var = 5
while var > 0:
    var = var -1
    if var == 3:
        continue
    print('Current variable value :', var)

Current variable value : 4
Current variable value : 2
Current variable value : 1
Current variable value : 0
```

It checks for certain condition when the condition is true, it executes the program. When control comes to continue statement exits the loop and comes back again to loop. When the number is equal to 3 it terminates from the loop and executes the remaining part.

4.7.   The Pass Statement

The pass statement is a null operation. The pass statement is used when the code is executed but not has been written. It is used when a statement is required syntactically but does not want any command or code to execute.

Syntax

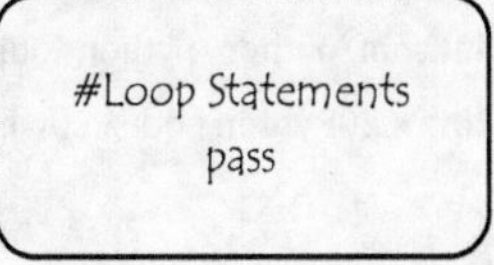

Example

for letter in 'Python':
if letter == 'h':
pass
print ('This is pass block')
print ('Current Letter:', letter)
print ("Good bye!")

Output

Current Letter: P
Current Letter: y
Current Letter: t

This is pass block
Current Letter: h
Current Letter: o
Current Letter: n
Good bye!

Summary

There are three different loops to perform repetitive tasks. For loops are best to iterate over a known sequence of elements. While loops are best when to operate while a certain condition is true. Continue, Break and Pass statements are executed after loops for further execution or for terminating the block. These loops will help to short the number of codes that wants to be written number of times.

References

[1]   https://www.programiz.com/python-programming/while-loop

[2]   https://www.tutorialspoint.com/python/python_while_loop.htm

[3]   https://www.programiz.com/python-programming/for-loop

[4]   https://www.tutorialspoint.com/python/python_for_loop.htm

[5]   https://www.tutorialspoint.com/python/python_continue_statement.htm

[6]   https://www.tutorialspoint.com/python/python_loop_control.htm#:~:text=The%20continue%20statement%20in%20Python,both%20while%20and%20for%20loops.

4.8.   Test Your Skill

Choose the Right Answer

1. ____________ statement is needed to control the flow of execution of the program.

    a)   Return

    b)   Control

    c)   if else

    d)   looping

2. ____________ loop is used when he/she do not know how many times to iterate.

    a)   While

    b)   Switch

    c)   do while

    d)   nested if

3. ______________ is the best example for while loop.

   a) Travelling in a bus

   b) sum of numbers

   c) Consulting the doctor

   d) checks for certain condition

4. The temperature =115 It checks a statement whether the 112 is ____________ 115.

   a) Less than

   b) equal to

   c) greater than or equal to

   d) greater than

5. Continue is a ____________ used in python.

   a) Variable

   b) Keyword

   c) Object

   d) scope

6. ______________ is a keyword that brings the program control out of the loop.

   a) Return

   b) end

   c) else

   d) break

7. ______________ loop repeats the control structure to efficiently.

   a) While

   b) For

   c) do while

   d) else if

8. Travelling in a bus the goes around and around until there are passengers in the bus is an example of ____________

   a) For statement

   b) loop

   c) exit

   d) control statement

9. ______________ is a loop which is blended with one or more loops.

    a) Nested loop

    b) for loop

    c) multiple elseif

    d) switch

10. ______________ Program executes the outer loop first

    a) While loop

    b) for loop

    c) nested loop

    d) if else

Answer the Following Briefly

1. Execute while loop with flowchart.

2. Characterize the applications of while loop.

3. Generate the real time example of for loop.

4. Explain the break statement?

5. Explain the nested loops?

CHAPTER 5

5. Functions

Learning Outcomes

- Describe the importance of functions in python.
- Call functions using actual parameters.
- To write functions that return multiple values with program.
- Understanding the use of local and global variable appropriately.

Importance of Function

- Function is pre-owned to bundle a set of instructions that are used repeatedly, because of their complexity a sub-program is called. This sub-program is a function.
- Function a piece of code which is important to carry out a specified task.

5.1.   Introduction

It is difficult to maintain a large-scale program and identification of the flow of the data is harder. Best way to optimize the program is divide and conquer method. It breaks the large program into smaller modules and call those modules repeatedly. Functions divides the larger program to smaller modules. Function also can compute a result value and specify parameters that serve as function inputs, which may differ each time when the code is executed. It is the basic program structure provided for maximizing code reuse and minimizing code redundancy.

Advantages of Functions

- Code reusability
- Managing the flow is easier
- Faster Execution

Rules for Defining Function

- Functions blocks begin with the keyword del followed by the function name and parentheses (()).
- Any input parameters or arguments should be placed within these parentheses. Parameters inside parenthesis can also be defined.
- The code block within every function starts with a colon (:) and is identified.
- The statement return exists a function, optionally passing back an expression to the caller.
- A return statement with no arguments is the same as return none.

Types of Function

Functions are divided into two types:

1. Built-in functions
2. User-defined functions

Built-in Functions

Built-in functions are several functions that are available for use. Some of the build in functions are mentioned below.

- abs () – returns absolute value of a number.

- all () – returns true when all elements in iterable is true.

- bin () – converts integer to binary string.

- bool () – converts a value to Boolean.

- chr () – returns a character from an integer.

- dict () – creates a dictionary.

- float () – returns floating point number from string, number.

User-defined Functions

Functions that are defined by the user to do specific task are user-defined functions.

Example

```
def add_numbers(x,y):
    sum = x + y
    return sum
num1 = 9
num2 = 6
print("The sum is",add_numbers(num1,num2))

The sum is 15
```

5.2. Syntax and Basics of a Function

A function are block of one or more statements executes when the particular function is called. Function provides better modularity for application and a high degree of code reusing. Syntax of the function are defined as follow.

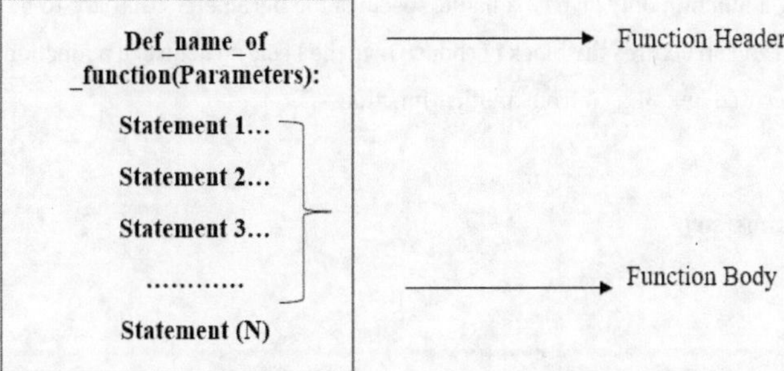

Function consists of two parts Header and Body. Header begins with **def** keyword. Keyword **def** defines the beginning of the function's definition. Name of the function should be followed by def keyword. Header may contain no. of parameters from 0-n. Parameters are called **Formal Parameters**. Parameters should be separated by comma if there are more than one parameter. Body of the function is block of multiple statements. Statements in the Body define the actions where functions need to perform.

Example

```
def Display():#Declaring the Function
    print("Welcome")
Display() #calling the Function

Welcome
```

Explanation

From the above program, functionDisplay () is created. It has no parameters. FunctionDisplay () is called and printed the statement "Welcome" inside the block.

Example

```
def my_func():
    x = 20
print("Value inside function:",x)
my_func()

Value inside function: 20
```

Explanation

From the above program, function My_Func() is created. It has no parameters. X variable is declared and printed when the function My_Func is called.

Calling a Function

Defining a function only gives it a name, specifies the parameters that are to be included in the function and structures the block of codes. Once the basic structure of a function is finalized it can be executed by calling it from another function.

Example

```
def printme(str);

  print str

   return;

   #Calling printme function

printme ("I am first call to user defined function")

   printme("Again second call to the same function")
```

Output

```
I am first call to user defined function
Again second call to the same function
```

Pass by Reference

All parameters(arguments) are passed by reference. It means when a change in parameter refers to within function, the change also reflects back in the calling function.

Example

```
def changeme( mylist ):

mylist. append ([1,2,3,4]):

  print "Values inside the function: ", mylist

   return

mylist = [10,20,30]:

changeme(mylist ):

print "Values outside the function: ", mylist
```

Output

```
Values inside the function: [10, 20, 30, [1, 2, 3, 4]]
Values outside the function: [10, 20, 30, [1, 2, 3, 4]]
```

5.3.   Use of a Function

Functions can be used in programming to club a set of instructions that you want to use repeatedly, because of the complexity, it is better to have a self-contained sub-program and call when needed. A function is a piece of code written to carry out a specified task. To carry out that specified task, the function may or might not need multiple inputs. When the task is carried out, the function will return one or more values depending on the code.

5.4.   Parameters and Arguments in a Function

Parameter and argument can be used for a passing information to the function.

A parameter is the variable listed inside the parentheses () in the function's definition.

An argument is the value that are sent to the function when it is called.

By default, a function should be called with the correct number of arguments, that is if your function expects 2 arguments, you have to call the function with 2 arguments, not more, and not less exactly two.

```
def my_function(fname, lname):
  print(fname + " " + lname)

my_function("Emil")
```

```
---------------------------------------------------------------
TypeError                        Traceback (most recent call last)
<ipython-input-3-49655f8043be> in <module>()
    2   print(fname + " " + lname)
    3
----> 4 my_function("Emil")

TypeError: my_function() missing 1 required positional argument: 'lname'
```

SEARCH STACK OVERFLOW

5.4.1. Positional Arguments

Python functions has two types of arguments.

- Positional Arguments.
- Keyword Arguments.

An **argument** is a variable or object passed as a input to a function. **Positional arguments** are nothing but **arguments** which need to be included in the proper **position** or order. When the function is called, first **positional argument** always needs to be listed first always. Positional arguments must be included in the correct order. The second positional argument needs to be listed second and the third positional argument listed third and so on.

From the above Example we will see how this function works.

```python
def emp(name, desc):
    """This function greets to
    the person with the provided message"""
    print("Hello", name + ', ' + desc)

emp("Monica", "Software Developer")
```

```
Hello Monica, Software Developer
```

From the above example emp details parameters are passed as name and desc and the function emp is called. The total parameter is 2 name and designation of the employee.

Now we will discuss about incorrect positions.

```python
def emp(name, desc):
    """This function greets to
    the person with the provided message"""
    print("Hello", name + ', ' + desc)

emp("Monica", )
```

```
---------------------------------------------------------------------------
TypeError                                 Traceback (most recent call last)
<ipython-input-3-1df012f88818> in <module>()
      4     print("Hello", name + ', ' + desc)
      5
----> 6 emp("Monica", )

TypeError: emp() missing 1 required positional argument: 'desc'
```


5.4.2. Keywords Arguments

An alternative to positional arguments are keyword arguments. A programmer can pass a keyword argument for a function by its respective parameter name than its position or order. When we call a function with certain values, these values will get assigned to the arguments according to their position. For example, in the above function emp (), when we called it as emp ("Monica", "Data Scientist") the value "Monica" gets assigned to name and "Data Scientist" assigned to designation of the employee. Python allows functions to be called using keyword arguments. When we call the functions, the position of the arguments can be changed. Following call the above function are all valid and produce the same result.

Syntax

Name_of_a_Function(pos_args, keyword1=value,keyword2=value2...

The above example will describe Keyword Argument, for the example of calculating the first mark in the class using Keyword argument.

```python
def my_function(child3, child2, child1):
    print("The class first is " + child3)

my_function(child1 = "Emil", child2 = "Tobias", child3 = "Linus")

The class first is Linus
```

Precaution for Keyword Arguments

1. Positional argument should not follow a keyword argument

   For example consider the following definition,

   Def Display(num1,num2):

Keyword should have its own values, its should not be like positional arguments.

When the programmer calls a functionDisplay() as Display(**30**,num3=10) but not as Display(num3=10,30) because the positional argument 30 should be in its proper position.

2. Programmer cannot duplicate an both keyword and positional argument

   From the above function

   def Display(num1,num2):

   cannot call as

   def Display(40,num2=40) this function will return a error.

5.4.3. Parameter with Default Values

Parameters within function definition can have default values. It allow function arguments as its default values. If the function is called without the argument, the argument will get its default value.

Python has a various way for representing syntax and default values for function arguments. Default values indicates that if function argument has no argument, it will take that value. If in default argument value which is passed during the function call.

The default value is assigned by using the **assignment (=) operator** of the form

***keyword name*=value**

For example, we have function called *student*. The function *student* contains 3-arguments ()out of those 2 arguments are assigned with default values. So, the function *student* accepts one required argument (*first name*), and rest of the two arguments are optional.

```python
def student(firstname, lastname ='Mark', standard ='Fifth'):
    print(firstname,lastname,'studies in', standard,'Standard')
student('paul')
```

```
paul Mark studies in Fifth Standard
```

From the above example the parameter first name as the required argument and last name and standard is considered as default values.

```python
def greet(name,msg="Welcome"):
    print("Hello",name,msg)
greet("amit")
```

```
Hello amit Welcome
```

Function greet() has a parameter name, msg. **name** do not have any default value and is compulsory during a function call and the **msg** has its default value called "**welcome'.**

Points to be Remember While Calling a Function

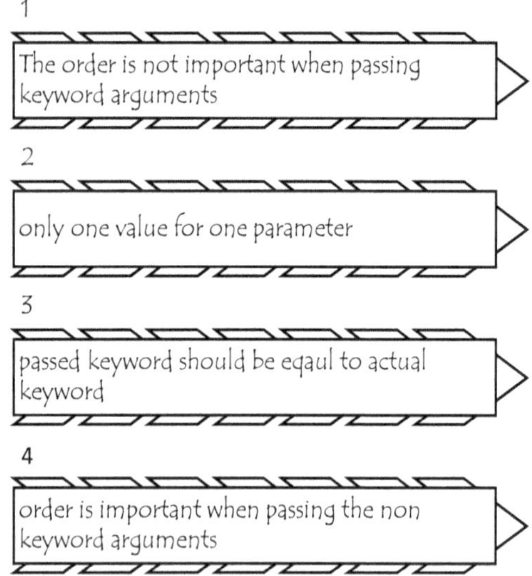

5.5. The Range () Function

The **range** () function will return a sequence of numbers, start from 0 (by default) and increments by 1 (by default), and stops before a specified number.

range (start, stop, step)

Parameter	Description
Start	(Optional)An integer number should be specified at which position it should start. (Default is 0)
Stop	(Mandatory)An integer number must be specified at which position it should stop
Step	(Optional) A specified integer number will increment. As a Default it will incremented as 1

5.5.1. Examples of Range () Function

From the below example we will understand how the range function will work without start and step parameter. There is no start and step function only stop parameter is defined as range (6).

```
x = range(6)
for n in x:
    print(n)

0
1
2
3
4
5
```

Figure: Range Function Without Optional Parameters

```
x = range(4,6)
for n in x:
    print(n)

4
5
```

Figure: Range Function with Optional Parameters

From the above example we will understand how the range function will work with start and step parameter. There is start and step function only stop parameter is defined as range (4,6).

5.6.   The Local and Global Scope of a Variable

The variables and parameters which are initialised within a function including the parameters, are existing in the function's local scope. Variables that exist in local scope are called as **Local Variables,** which can be access only within that function. Variables which are assigned outside the function are said to be global scope. Variables inside the global scope are global variables can be accessed globally.

```
p=input("Enter a number");
def Disp():
    s=input("Enter a number")
    print('The value of a global variable p:',p)
    print('The value of a local variable s:',s)
Disp()

Enter a number21
Enter a number23
The value of a global variable p: 21
The value of a local variable s: 23
```

Explanation

The function disp () has a local variable sand a global variable p has its access throughout the function but the local variable s has its access only within the scope.

5.6.1. Reading Global Variables From a Local Scope

Global variable are defined outside of the function generally on the top of the function. The lifetime of Global variable's values lifetime of the program and they can be accessed within any of the function defined. A global variable can be accessed by any function. The global variable is available throughout the entire program after its declaration. It can be accessed through the local function.

```
p=input("Enter a number");
def Disp():
    s=input("Enter a number")
    print('The value of a global variable p:',p)
    print('The value of a local variable s:',s)
Disp()

Enter a number21
Enter a number23
The value of a global variable p: 21
The value of a local variable s: 23
```

Explanation

From the above example the p is a global variable which is declared on the top of the function. It is called when the function Disp() is called. Scope of the global variable is valid until the function Disp is called.

5.6.2. Local and Global Variables with the Same Name

A program can have the **same name** for both **local and global variables** but the value of a **local variable** inside a function will take preference. Local variable will take a highest preference. For example, the below program contains both local and global variable with the same name but at the time of execution the value for local variable is executed. A built-in function Global () return a dictionary object and their values. With the help of name of the variable as a key the value can be accessed and modified.

Explanation

Two local and global variable has the same name g but the local variable takes its higher preference.

5.6.3. The Global Statement

The **global** statement is a declaration which hold the entire current code block. The mentioned identifiers in the code block are set as global by default. While *using* global names is automatic if they are not defined in the local scope and if they have global keyword to the variable it's considered as global by default. *Assigning* global names without a keyword global would be impossible.

$$\boxed{\text{global\_stmt: "global" identifier ("," identifier)*}}$$

Note for the Programmer is the global is a directive to the parser. It applies only to code parsed at the same time as the global statement.

```
c = 0 # global variable
def add():
    global c
    c = c + 2 # increment by 2
    print("Inside add():", c)
add()
print("In main:", c)

Inside add(): 2
In main: 2
```

Explanation

From the above example, the variable c is declared as global with the keyword global.

```python
def myfunction():
  global x
  x = "hello"

#execute the function:
myfunction()
#x should now be global, and accessible in the global scope.
print(x)

hello
```

5.7.   The Return Statement

The return statement is used for returning a value from the function. It is also used to return a value from a function i.e. breaking out from a function. If the return statement is without any expression the value returned from the function is none. It cannot execute outside the function.

Syntax

def fun():

statements.

....

return [expression]

```python
def get_even(numbers):
    even_nums = [num for num in numbers if not num % 2]
    return even_nums
get_even([1, 2, 3, 4, 5, 6])

[2, 4, 6]
```

Explanation

From the above example ,the function will return the even numbers from the given numbers. It uses for loop to find the even numbers and return the value.

```python
def mul(a, b):
    result = a * b
    return result

mul(2, 2)

4
```

Explanation

From the above example, the function mul will return the product of the two numbers from the given numbers. Function mul() is passed with two arguments a,b and its value are 2,2.

5.7.1. Returning Multiple Values

It is possible to return multiple values from a function.

```python
def calc_arith_op(num1,num2):
    return num1*num2,num1/num2
print("",calc_arith_op(10,20))
```

```
(200, 0.5)
```

Explanation

In the program, two parameters called num1, num2 are passed to a function **calc_arith_op()**. In the body of the function the return statement computes product and division of two number num1, num2. Finally, the return statement returns value of the both product and division of the two numbers.

5.7.2. Assign Returned Multiple Values to Variable(s)

It is possible for a function to perform a certain operation, return multiple values and also assign the returned multiple values to multiple variables.

Write a program to return multiple values from a function.

```python
def compute(num1):
    print("Number=",num1)
    return num1*num1,num1*num1*num1
square, cube=compute(4)
print("square=",square,"Cube=",cube)
```

```
Number= 4
square= 16 Cube= 64
```

Explanation

The number is passed to the function compute (). The return statement calculates the square and cube of passed number. After computing, it returns both the values at the same time. Returned square of number 4 is assigned to Square and the returned cube of number is assigned to Cube.

5.8.   Recursive Functions

In program there may be a certain situation to call the program itself. Python supports the recursive function that is a function which call itself repeatedly, thus a function is called as recursive if a statement within a body of the function calls itself.

Syntax

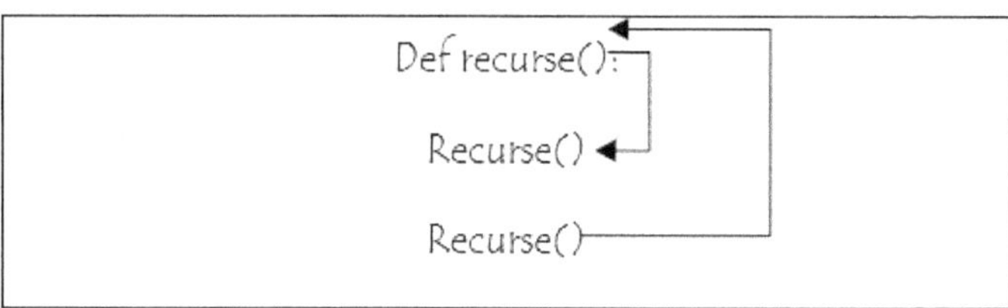

Let us consider an example of recursion. For example, if we want to calculate a factorial for a given number. As all of us know factorial of a given number is calculated by the product of all integers between and the numbers are defined as n*(n-1)!.

Formula for calculating factorial of 5.

5! =5*(4)!

5*4*(3)!

5*4*3*(2)!

5*4*3*2*(1)!

=120

Write a program to find a factorial of a number.

```python
def factorial(n):
    if n==0:
        return 1
    return n*factorial(n-1)
print(factorial(5))

120
```

Explanation

From the above example the factorial() is a recursive function. The number is passed to function factorial (), when the function factorial is called it repeatedly invokes itself. Every time a function is invoked the number is decremented by 1(n-1), and the product of each integer 5,4,3,2,1 is calculated. finally, the output is printed as 120.

Write a program to fin Fibonacci series using recursion.

```
def fib(n):
  if n==0:
    return 1
  if n==1:
    return 1
  return fib(n-1)+fib(n-2)
print("the value of 6th fibonaci series=",fib(6))

the value of 6th fibonaci series= 13
```

Advantages and Disadvantages

Advantages	Disadvantages
• It makes the code simple	• Sometimes the logic is hard to follow
• It breaks the complex task to a simple sub program	• It is expensive and involves more time
• Recursion is easier than nested iteration	• Hard to debug

5.9.   The Lambda Function

Lambda function is named after Greek letter **λ(Lambda).** It is also known as anonymous function. These kinds of functions are not for a name but only to code to execute which is associated to it.

Syntax for Lambda Functions

Name = Lambda(variable): Code

For example, consider a simple program to calculate square of number using a simple function.

```
def func(x):
  return x*x
print(func(3))

9
```

Explanation

The func () has one parameter x it will return a x*x when the function is passed with the value of x. it will print the value of x.

The above is example how it executes without the lambda function.

With Lambda Function

The Same Program is Executed Using Lambda Function

```
square=lambda x:x*x*x
print(square(3))

27
```

Explanation

Thus the above program explain how lambda function is used to calculate the square of the number passed as a value in the function. The square=lambda x:x*x*x creates a lambda function that takes a single argument and return the square of the number.

Uses of Lambda Function

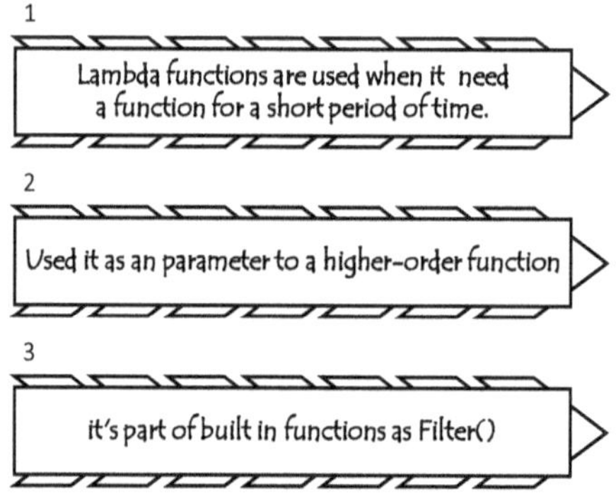

Summary

The core ideas behind functions are explained. The syntax and operations of def statements, a function calling expressions are explained. Key concepts of related to functions are reported. Arguments are passed into function by reference. Advanced function related concepts like lambda function, recursive functions gathered. Scope of variable and global variables are exercised with examples.

References

[1]   https://www.programiz.com/python-programming/function

[2]   https://www.programiz.com/python-programming/anonymous-function#:~:text=We%20use%20lambda%20functions%20when,filter()%20%2C%20%20map()%20etc.

[3]   https://www.programiz.com/python-programming/examples/fibonacci-recursion

[4]   https://www.geeksforgeeks.org/g-fact-41-multiple-return-values-in-python/

[5]   https://www.geeksforgeeks.org/g-fact-41-multiple-return-values-in-python/

[6]   https://realpython.com/python-return-statement/

5.10. Test Your Skill

Choose the Right Answer

1. ____________ consists of two parts Header and Body.

    a) Statement

    b) para

    c) syntax

    d) function

2. Header begins with ___________ keyword.

    a) If

    b) else

    c) def

    d) as

3. An/A ___________ is a variable or object passed as an input to a function.

    a) Keyword

    b) constant

    c) syntax

    d) Argument

4. Variables that exist in local scope are called as ___________ Variables.

    a) Inner

    b) local

    c) inbound

    d) scope

5. The ___________ statement is used for returning a value from the function.

    a) Return

    b) function

    c) exceptional

    d) global

6. An alternative to positional arguments is ______________ arguments.

    a) keyword

    b) Parameter

    c) functional

    d) required

7. It is possible to return multiple values from a function.

    a) True

    b) false

    c) either true or false

    d) none

8. An argument is the value that are sent to the function when it is called.

    a) Operations

    b) function

    c) variable

    d) loop

9. Lambda function is named after Greek letter ______________

    a) $

    b) &

    c) λ

    d) *

10. The ______________ statement is a declaration which hold the entire current code block.

    a) Return

    b) multiple

    c) global

    d) local

Answer the Following Briefly

1. List the syntax and basics of a function.

2. Outline the Parameters and Arguments in a Function?

3. Illustrate the necessary Precaution for Keyword Arguments?

4. Examine return statement.

5. Discuss about recursive function?

6. Lists, Tuples, Sets and Dictionaries

Learning Outcomes

- Depict the Python Lists, Tuples, Sets and Dictionaries, its functions and Operations.
- Demonstrate Zip () and Zip (*) functions.
- Membership Operations in Sets.
- Illustrate Nested Dictionaries.

Container is an entity which contains multiple data items. It is also known as a collection. Python has following container data types:

Lists

Tuples

Sets

Dictionaries

Container data types are also known as compound data types.

6.1.   Lists

List is an ordered sequence of items. It is one of the most used data type in Python. A list is that items in a list need not be of the same type. List are somewhat similar to arrays in C. But one difference is that all the items belonging to a list can be of different data type.

6.1.1.   Creating Lists

Items are separated by commas are enclosed within brackets[ ]. The values stored in a list can be accessed using the slice operator ([ ] and [:]) with indexes starting at 0 in the beginning of the list and ending with -1. The plus (+) sign is the list concatenation operator, and the asterisk (*) is the repetition operator.

Example Program

```
A_list = ['xyz',565,2.54,'Jack',98.2]
B_list = [100, 'jack']
print (A_list)
print (A_list[1:3])
print(A_list[2:])
print(B_list * 2)
print(A_list + B_list)
```

['xyz', 565, 2.54, 'Jack', 98.2]

[565, 2.54]

[2.54, 'Jack', 98.2]

[100, 'jack', 100, 'jack']

['xyz', 565, 2.54, 'Jack', 98.2, 100, 'jack']

You can update single or multiple elements of lists by giving the slice on the left-hand side of the assignment operator.

Example Program

```
# Demo of List update
list=['xyz',565,2.54,'Jack',98.2]
print(" Item at position 3=", list[3])
list[3]='Sam'
print("Item at position 3=" ,list[3])
print("Item at Position 0 and 1 is", list[0],list[1])
list[0]=20; list[1]='PQR'
print("Item at Position 0 and 1 is", list[0],list[1])
```

Output

```
Item at position 3= Jack
Item at position 3= Sam
Item at Position 0 and 1 is xyz 565
Item at Position 0 and 1 is 20 PQR
```

Two methods are used to remove an item from a list. We can del statement or remove () method.

Example Program

```
#Demo of List deletion
list=['xyz',565,2.54,'Jack',98.2]
print(list)
del list[2]
print ("List after deletion: ", list)
```

Output

```
['xyz', 565, 2.54, 'Jack', 98.2]
List after deletion: ['xyz', 565, 'Jack', 98.2]
```

6.1.2. Built-in Functions

1. Syntax :len(list) – It gives the total length of the list.

Example Program

```
#Demo of len(list)
list=['xyz',565,2.54,'Jack',98.2]
print(len(list))
```

Output

```
5
```

2. Syntax :Max(list) – It returns item the list with maximum value

Example Program

```
#Demo of max(list)
A_list = [1000,565,2.54,178,98.2]
B_list = [100, 234,67]
print("Maximum value in : ",A_list, "is" ,max(A_list) )
print("Maximum value in : ",B_list, "is" ,max(B_list) )
```

Output

```
Maximum value in :  [1000, 565, 2.54, 178, 98.2] is 1000
Maximum value in :  [100, 234, 67] is 234
```

3. Syntax :min(list) – It returns item from the list with minimum value

Example Program

```
#demo of min(list)
A_list = [1000,565,2.54,178,98.2]
B_list = [100, 234,67]
print("Minimum value in : ",A_list, "is" ,min(A_list) )
print("Minimum value in : ",B_list, "is" ,min(B_list) )
```

Output

```
Minimum value in :  [1000, 565, 2.54, 178, 98.2] is 2.54
Minimum value in :  [100, 234, 67] is 67
```

6.1.3. Built-in Methods

1. Syntax:list.append(obj) – This method is used to append an object obj passed to the existing list.

Example Program

```
#Demo of list.append(obj)
list=['xyz',565,2.54,'Jack',98.2]
print("Before Append: ", list)
list.append('Poly')
print("After Append:", list)
```

Output

```
Before Append:  ['xyz', 565, 2.54, 'Jack', 98.2]
After Append: ['xyz', 565, 2.54, 'Jack', 98.2, 'Poly']
```

2. Syntax:list.count(obj) - It returns how many times the object *obj* appears in a list.

Example Program

```
#Demo of list.count(obj)
list = ['xyz',565,2.54,'Jack',98.2, 565,'Tom',100, 565]
print("The number of times", 565,  "appears in", list, " = ", list.count(565))
```

Output

```
The number of times 565 appears in ['xyz', 565, 2.54, 'Jack', 98.2,
565, 'Tom', 100, 565] = 3
```

3. Syntax:list.remove(obj) - It removes object obj from the list

Example Program

```
#Demo of list.remove(obj)
list=['xyz',565,2.54,'Jack',98.2, 565,'Tom',100, 565]
list.remove('xyz')
print(list)
```

Output

```
[565, 2.54, 'Jack', 98.2, 565, 'Tom', 100, 565]
```

4. Syntax:list.index(obj) – It returns index of the object obj if found, otherwise raise an exception indicating that value does not exist.

Example Program

```
#Demo of list.index(obj)
list=['xyz',565,2.54,'Jack',98.2]
print(list.index(2.54))
```

6.2. Tuples

The ordered and immutable objects are collected together within the curved brackets ( ) to form a Tuple, is a standard Python data structure. The objects of a tuple are sequenced and are separated using the commas.

Example

    tup_1 = ( )
    tup_2 = ("apple",)
    tup_3 = ('a', 'b', 'c', 'd', 'e')
    tup_4 = ((1, 2), (3, 4))

The addition of a comma is a mandatory process while composing a tuple, even though the tuple contains a single object.

6.2.1. Creating Tuples

The tuples are created using any number of variables of different data types such as integer, float, string, etc. The variables are separated by commas which is mandatory while the parentheses are not. Such, the tuples without parentheses are known as 'Tuple Packing'.

Example

    tup_1 = (1, 'a', 1.8)
    tup_2 = (1, 2, 3)

6.2.2. The Tuple ( ) Function

The Python uses tuple ( ) function, a built-in function to create a tuple with a sequence of iterator objects. With iterables, a corresponding tuple is formed and without iterables, an empty tuple. The tuple() can covert a given list into a tuple.

Syntax

    tuple (iterable)

Example Program

```
l = ["1, 2, 3, 4, 5"]
print ("list l = ", l)
print ("l = ",type(l))
t= tuple (l)
print ("tuple t = ", t)
print("t = ", type(t))
```

> list l = ['1,2,3,4,5']
>
> l = <class 'list'>
>
> tuple t = ('1,2,3,4,5',)
>
> t = <class 'tuple'>

6.2.3. Inbuilt Functions for Tuples

The Python built-in function used for tuples are:

- **Length of the tuple**

> Syntax: len (tuple_1)

The len() function returns the length of a particular tuple. That is, the count of the number of the elements present in the tuple is returned.

Example Program

> t1 = (12,"ab", "one", 230)
>
> t2 = (34, "two",100)
>
> print("Length of tuple t1 = ",len(t1))
>
> print("Length of tuple t2 = ",len(t2))

Output

> Length of tuple t1 = 4
>
> Length of tuple t2 = 3

- **Maximum in the tuple**

> Syntax: max (tuple_1)

To find the maximum value of the elements, the max ( ) function has been called.

Example Program

> print(max(1,34,4,56))
>
> print(max("ab","a","xz","fg"))

Output

> 56
>
> xz

- **Minimum in the tuple**

> Syntax: min (tuple_1)

To find the minimum value of the elements, the min( ) function has been used.

Example Program

                print(min(1,34,4,56))

                print(min("ab","a","xz","fg"))

Output

                1

                a

- **Conversion**

                Syntax: tuple (seq)

To convert a given list into a tuple, the tuple(seq) has been used.

Example Program

                print (tuple([1,2,3,4,5]))

Output

                (1, 2, 3, 4, 5)

6.2.4. *Indexing and Slicing*

Indexing

The indexes of the tuples are much similar to that of the strings. The index of the tuples begins with the value of 0 and continues on. The perform indexing or slicing on the tuples, the square brackets are used along with the index values.

Example

                t = (1, 2, 3, 4, 5) here t[0] = 1, t[2] =3 , ... t[4] = 5.

The index value given within the square brackets represents the value in the tuple that needs to be accessed.

Case 1: If the value given as index is positive, then counting starts from the left to obtain that particular index from the tuple. The counting starts with zero and moves on.

Case 2: if the index value given is negative, then the counting starts from the right to find the index of the tuple. Here the counting starts with not zero but -1 and moves on.

Positive indexing	Negative Indexing
t [0] = 1	t [-5] = 1
t[1] = 2	t [-4] = 2
...	...
t [4] =5	t [-1] = 5

Example Program

```
t = (1, 2, 3, 4, 5)
print("Indexing:")
print(t[1])
print(t[2])
print(t[-2])
print(t[-1])
```

Output

```
Indexing:
2
3
4
5
```

Slicing

To access a particular part of the tuple, the slicing operator has been used. The starting values for slicing and the end value are specified within the square bracket with colon (:).

Syntax: tuple_1[start: stop: increment]

Example Program

```
x =("abc","cde","efg","ghi","ijk")
print("[1:] = ", x[1:])  # 1st to the end (no value after the 1st colon)
print("[:2] = ", x[:2])  # start to 2nd
print("[1:3] = ", x[1:3]) # 1st to 3rd
print("[::2] = ", x[::2]) # start to end with stepsize of 2
print("[::-1] = ", x[::-1])
```

Output

```
[1:] = ('cde', 'efg', 'ghi', 'ijk')
[:2] = ('abc', 'cde')
[1:3] = ('cde', 'efg')
[::2] = ('abc', 'efg', 'ijk')
[::-1] = ('ijk', 'ghi', 'efg', 'cde', 'abc')
```

i). When the tuple has to be traversed backwards, the increment index value has been given as -1.

ii). To get and skip to the second elements every time, the increment step value has been set as -2.

Python Slice Object

The slice object used in Python is a substitution method for the above discussed colon syntax to slice the objects off the tuple.

Example Program

```
x = (1, 2, 3, 4, 5, 6, 7, 8, 9,)

s = slice(2,5)

print(s)

print(x[s])

print(x[slice(3,7)])

print(x[slice(2,-2)])

print(x[slice(1,-3)])

print(x[slice(1,6)])
```

Output

```
slice (2, 5, none)

(3, 4, 5)

(4, 5, 6, 7)

(3, 4, 5, 6, 7)

(2, 3, 4, 5, 6)

(2, 3, 4, 5, 6)
```

6.2.5. Operations on Tuples

The following are the operations that are applied on the Python tuples:

- **Tuple Concatenation**

Two tuples are united together to form a single tuple through the process of concatenation by using the + operator.

Example Program

```
g = ("Priya", "Usha", "Ramya")
b = ("Aun", "Varun", "kumar")
names = g + b
print ("Names = ",names)
t = (1, 2, 3, 4)
t = t + (5,)
print("Numbers = ", t)
```

Output

```
Names =  ('Priya', 'Usha', 'Ramya', 'Arun', 'Varun', 'kumar')
Numbers =  (1, 2, 3, 4, 5)
```

- **Tuple Repetition**

To have the same tuple to be multiplied many times to form a single tuple, the multiplication operator * has been used.

Example Program

```
g = ("Priya", "Usha", "Ramya")
g = g * 2
print(g)
n = (2,4,6,8)
m = n * 3
print (m)
```

Output

```
('Priya', 'Usha', 'Ramya', 'Priya', 'Usha', 'Ramya')
(2, 4, 6, 8, 2, 4, 6, 8, 2, 4, 6, 8)
```

- **Tuple Contains**

To find out whether a given element is present within a tuple, the in operator has been used. If the element is present, then the Boolean value of TRUE has been returned else FALSE has been returned.

Example Program

```
n = (1, 2, 3, 4, 5)
f = 1 in n
print ("Is 1 in n ? : ",f)
s = 6 in n
print ("Is 6 in n ? : ",s)
```

> Is 1 in n? : True
>
> Is 6 in n? : False

- **Tuple Not Contains**

If a particular element is not present, then the not in operator returns the TRUE Boolean value else the FALSE value has been returned.

Example Program

> n = (1, 2, 3, 4, 5)
>
> f = 1 in n
>
> print ("Is 1 not in n ? : ",f)
>
> s = 6 in n
>
> print ("Is 6 not in n ? : ",s)

Output

> Is 1 in n? : False
>
> Is 6 in n? : True

- **Tuple Nesting**

The nesting operation is the process of storing and placing of one or more tuples inside a tuple.

Example Program

> a = (1, 2, 3, 4, 5)
>
> b = (6, 7, 8, 9, 10)
>
> n = (a,b)
>
> print ("Nesting \n",n)

Output

Nesting

((1, 2, 3, 4, 5), (6, 7, 8, 9, 10))

6.2.6. *Passing Variable Length Arguments to Tuples*

Example Program

```
def choose (a, b):
  return a<b
choice = choose (5,6)
print(choice)
```

Output

> True

This is a simple comparison program to find which of the element is greater. Thus, the comparison function holds only two arguments. But, if suppose a situation arises to handle more number of arguments to this function. To compare more number of arguments or passing an unknown or undefined number of arguments to a function, Python aids us to create a function that is capable of processing multiple numbers of arguments. Such function is known as **Function with Variable Length Arguments**.

Syntax

```
def function (*arguments):

    ...

    body of the function

    ...

    return
```

The variable that are prefixed with the Asterisk (*) symbol holds the values of the multiple arguments. The function with the Variable Length Arguments is proficient to accept an unknown or pre-determined number of arguments as the inputs.

Example Program

```
def choose(*n):
    choice = n[0]
    for x in n:
        if x> choice:
            choice = x
    return choice
        print("Maximum value:")
        choose(56,47,38, 78, 67,87,12)
```

Output

```
Maximum value:
87
```

The Variable Length Arguments must be followed by a named argument, yet the argument should not represent its position.

6.2.7. Lists and Tuples

Lists and Tuples are known standard data types of Python for the sequential data format. They are much similar to the array of other popular programming languages such as C or C++. Even lists and tuples are related to each other yet with the following differences.

	Lists	Tuples
1.	A sequential collection of data with the square brackets [ ]	An ordered data set within the curved brackets ( )
2.	The list contains homogeneous data, ie only the objects of same data type.	Tuple is made of heterogeneous data set, different data formats are accepted.
3.	List is known for its mutable or dynamic state.	Tuples are immutable, stable, can't be change.
4.	Performance is comparatively low.	Due to fast iteration, the tuples works as a performance booster.
5.	Lists are not able to be used as a key for a dictionary.	Tuples are used as the key for the dictionaries.
6.	Since the lists are mutable, the code has no security.	Due to the immutable property, codes are safer and the program is write-protected.
7.	Lists consume more memory.	Tuples are more optimistic in terms of space (memory) and time.
8.	Exception rises quite often while working with the lists.	Exception handling is rare while working with tuples.

6.2.8. Sort Tuples

i).   **Sorting tuples using sorted ( )**–Tuples can be sorted by using the built in function sorted ( );

Syntax: sorted ( )

Example Program

```
n = (4, 5,7,3,8,1,6,9,2)
            print("Sorted Tuple: \n")
                print(sorted(n))
print(type(n))
            print(tuple(sorted(n)))
```

Output

```
Sorted Tuple:

[1, 2, 3, 4, 5, 6, 7, 8, 9]

<class 'tuple'>

(1, 2, 3, 4, 5, 6, 7, 8, 9)
```

ii).   **Sorting tuples using sorted ( ) and key**– Tuples don't have prepared sort ( ) function due their immutable feature. Thus, the tuples cannot call the sort ( ) function directly. Thus the sorted ( ) function uses a key, a keyword argument according to which the sorting process takes place.

Example Program

```
def last(n):

    return n[m]

def sort(tuples):

    return sorted(tuples,key = last)

a= [(34,45,67),(45,18,21),(89,98,56)]

m= 1

print("Sorted:")

print(sort(a))
```

Output

```
Sorted:

[(45, 18, 21), (34, 45, 67), (89, 98, 56)]
```

iii).   Sorting tuples using sort ( ) and lambda

Sort () takes lambda (), a Python built-in function to sort the list of tuples.

Example Program

```
def tuple(x):

    x.sort(key = lambda X:X[0])

    return x

x = [("ten", 10), ("five", 5), ("twenty", 20),

    ("fifteen", 15)]

print(tuple(x)
```

Output

```
[('fifteen', 15), ('five', 5), ('ten', 10), ('twenty', 20)]
```

Sorting Tuples Using Bubble Sort

Bubble sorting method uses a nested loop to access the first element of given tuples in a list. This method is called as in-place method of sorting.

Example Program

```
def Sort_Tuple(tup):
  n = len(tup)
  for i in range(0, n):
      for j in range(0, n-i-1):
          if (tup[j][1] > tup[j + 1][1]):
              temp = tup[j]
              tup[j]= tup[j + 1]
              tup[j + 1]= temp
  return tup
tup =[(2,4),(1,3),(6,8),(9,11),(4,5)]
print(Sort_Tuple(tup))
```

Output

```
Sorted Tuple:
[(1, 3), (2, 4), (4, 5), (6, 8), (9, 11)]
```

iv).   Sorting tuples using Itemgetter ( )

To sort a list of tuples based on any of tuple element, that a particular tuple index. The Itemgetter () is a well known efficacy while working in a web development domain.

Example Program

```
from operator import itemgetter
t = [(4,5,1), (8,7,4),(6,3,7)]
print("Original Tuple:"+str(t))
n =1
t.sort(key = itemgetter(n))
print("Sorted Tuple:"+str(t))
```

Output

```
Original Tuple:[(4, 5, 1), (8, 7, 4), (6, 3, 7)]
Sorted Tuple:[(6, 3, 7), (4, 5, 1), (8, 7, 4)]
```

6.2.9.   *The Zip ( ) Function*

The Zip ( ) function is a built-in function in Python which use to return a Zip object. A Zip object is an iterator of tuples which pairs the first element of each tuple and second element of the each tuple together and continues so on with each elements of tuples respectively. In other words, the zip ( ) function maps similar index of two or more tuples to form a list of tuples. The function is more effective in printing multiple consecutive and equivalent elements from various iterators previously.

Syntax

zip (iterator_1, iterator_2, ..., iterator_n)

Example Program

```
a = (1,3,5,7,9)

b = (2,4,6,8)

n = zip(a,b)

print("Zip object for a and b:")

print(n)
```

Output

```
Zip object for a and b:

<zip object at 0x7fa92f99e088>
```

6.2.10. The Inverse Zip (*) Function

The inverse zip (*) function is an undo function of the Zip ( ) function. The tuples zipped together are unzipped here.

Syntax

zip (*)

Example Program

```
a = (1,3,5,7,9)

b = (2,4,6,8)

n = zip(a,b)

print("Zip object for a and b:")

print(n)

print ("Inverse Zip for n:")

print(*n)
```

Output

```
Zip object for a and b:

<zip object at 0x7fa92f9a2f08>

Inverse Zip for n:

(1, 2) (3, 4) (5, 6) (7, 8)
```

6.2.11. More Examples on Zip (*) Function

Example Program

Program to print the Employee names with their salary using Inverse Zip function

```
name = ("Arun","Varun", "kirun","Mike")
salary = (15000,8000,10000,12000)
emp = zip(name,salary)
print("Employee name with Salary:")
print(*emp)
```

Output

```
Employee name with Salary:
('Arun', 15000) ('Varun', 8000) ('kirun', 10000) ('Mike', 12000)
```

Example Program

Program using zip and *zip function

```
v = ["a","e","i","o","u"]
c = ["b","c","d","f","g","h"]
z= zip(v,c)
print("Inverse Zip",*z)
```

Output

```
Inverse Zip ('a', 'b') ('e', 'c') ('i','d') ('o', 'f') ('u', 'g')
```

6.2.12. More Programs on Tuples

Example Program

Program to print a tuple in a reverse by using Slicing Operator

```
aTuple = (10, 20, 30, 40, 50)
aTuple = aTuple[::-1]
print(aTuple)
```

Output

```
Reversing a Tuple:
(9, 8, 7, 6, 5, 4, 3, 2, 1)
```

Example Program

Program to print the number of elements in a given tuple

```
tup = (1,3,4,3,5,6,7,2,4,6,1,5,4,7,3,6,5,3,2)
print("No. of '3s' in this tuple:",tup.count(3))
print("No. of '6s' in this tuple:",tup.count(6))
print("No. of '1s' in this tuple:",tup.count(1))
```

Output

> No. of '3s' in this tuple: 4
>
> No. of '6s' in this tuple: 3
>
> No. of '1s' in this tuple: 2

6.3. Sets

A Python set is a collection of elements that are unordered, immutable and has the hash table, a data structure as the foundation. The elements within the set cannot be subjected to any replications and there is no index values assigned to them. A Python set as like Python list can be mutable as a whole but the elements within a particular set are outlawed to any sort of modification.

6.3.1. Creating Sets

- The set is unordered collection of elements by placing them within the set or curly brackets { }.

Ex: x = {1, 2, 3, 4, 5}

- The **set () function**, a standard Python built-in function used to create a set.

Example Program

```
x = [1,2,3,4,5]
print("Set x = ",set(x))
a = print("Set a = ", set(["a","b","c"]))
```

Output

```
Set x = {1, 2, 3, 4, 5}
Set a = {'a', 'b', 'c'}
```

Accessing Values from a Set

Since there is no indexing in Python set, a particular element access is not possible. The only possibility is to have a list of the entity elements by using the looping statements.

Example Program

```
x = set (("Apple", "Banana", "Citrus"))
print ("Set x     =", x)
for i in x:
  print(i)
```

Output

```
Set x = {'Banana', 'Apple', 'Citrus'}
Banana
Apple
Citrus
```

Updating Elements in a Set

To add an element to a given set, the add() function has been executed.

Example Program

```
x = set (("Apple", "Banana","Citrus"))
print ("Set x =", x)
x. add("Dragon Fruit")
print("Updated Set x =",x)
```

Output

```
Set x = {'Banana', 'Apple', 'Citrus'}
Updated Set x = {'Banana', 'Dragon Fruit', 'Apple', 'Citrus'}
```

Deleting an Element in a Set

To delete an element from a given set, the discard () function has been used.

Example Program

```
x = set (("Apple", "Banana","Citrus"))
print ("Set x =", x)
x. discard("Citrus")
print("New Set x =",x)
```

Output

```
Set x = {'Banana', 'Apple', 'Citrus'}
New Set x = {'Banana', 'Apple'}
```

To clear the entire set by deleting all the set elements by leaving an empty set, the clear ( ) function has been subjected.

Example Program

```
x =set(('Banana', 'Apple', 'Citrus'))
print("Set x =", x)
x.clear()
print("Set :",x)
x.add("fruits")
print("set: ",x)
```

Output

```
Set x = {'Banana', 'Apple', 'Citrus'}
Set : set()
set:  {'fruits'}
```

6.3.2. *The Set in and Not in Operator*

The membership operators namely in and not in are used to check whether a value exists within a given set or not. It is one the major advantage of using the sets.

- In operator: Returns the Boolean value of TRUE, if expect value presents within the set else FALSE.

- Not in operator: Returns the Boolean value of TRUE if the particular value is not present within the set else FALSE.

Example Program

```
A = { 1, 2,3,4, 5}
B = {2,4,6,8}
print ("Is 3 in Set A? : ",3 in A)
print ("Is 3 in Set B? : ",3 in B)
print ("Is 3 not in B? : ",3 not in A)
print ("Is 3 not in B? : ",3 not in B)
```

Output

```
Is 3 in Set A? :  True
Is 3 in Set B? :  False
Is 3 not in B? :  False
Is 3 not in B? :  True
```

6.3.3. *The Python Set Class*

Set class module contains the construction and manipulation process that are subjected on the set attributes. The general function performed using the set classes are:

   i). Membership evaluating

  ii). Duplicating Deletion

 iii). Mathematic set operation (∩, ∪, -)

Set class involves in every application and supports every operation expect the _hash_ () method. To implement the set class, the dictionaries (a standard Python data type) have been used.

6.3.4. *Set Operations*

Alike the mathematic Set, a Python has the following operations:

  i). **Union Operation $A \cup B$** – Like OR operation, the union operation adds the given two sets to form a single set. If A and B are the two sets, there are combined together to form a set with unique elements and omitting repetitions. In terms of membership operation, the union of A and B is the collective set of all the elements **in** either of the sets.

Example Program

```
A = {1,2,3,4,5}

B = {2,4,6,8}

C = {1, 3, 5,7}

union = A | B

print("Union of A and B:",union)

union_1 = B.union(C)

print("Union of B and C:",union_1)
```

Output

```
Union of A and B: {1, 2, 3, 4, 5, 6, 8}

Union of B and C: {1, 2, 3, 4, 5, 6, 7, 8}
```

ii). **Intersection of sets A ∩ B** –The intersection accounts the common elements from set A and B. As per the membership function, the intersection of A and B is the collective set of all the elements **in** both of the sets.

Example Program

```
A = {1,2,3,4,5}

B = {2,4,6,8}

C = {1, 3, 5,7}

Inter = A & B

print("Intersection of A and B:",Inter)

inter_1 = B.intersection(C)

print("Intersection of B and C:",inter_1)

print ("Intersection of C and A:",C.intersection(A))
```

Output

```
Intersection of A and B: {2, 4}

Intersection of B and C: set ()

Intersection of C and A: {1, 3, 5}
```

iii). **Difference of sets A – B** – The difference among the set A and B are calculated here. A set has been created with the unique elements of Set A and none common from the set B. By the membership operation, the difference of A and B produce a set with all elements **in** A and **not in** B.

Example Program

A = {1,2,3,4,5}

B = {2,4,6,8}

C = {1, 3, 5,7}

Diff = A - B

print("Difference of A and B:",Diff)

diff_1 = B.difference(C)

print("Union of B and C:",diff_1)

diff_2 = C.difference(B)

print("Union of C and B:",diff_2)

Output

Difference of A and B: {1, 3, 5}

Union of B and C: {8, 2, 4, 6}

Union of C and B: {1, 3, 5, 7}

Other operators' implements on the sets are:

S. No	Operators	Functions
1.	in A	Containment checking
2.	not in B	Non- Containment Checking
3.	A == B	A equivalent to B
4.	A != B	A not- equivalent to B
5.	A < B	A is a proper subset of B
6.	A > B	A is a proper superset of B
7.	A<= B	A is a subset of B
8.	A>= B	A is a superset of B
9.	A | B	$A \cup B$
10.	A & B	$A \cap B$
11.	A – B	Set of elements in A and not in B
12.	A ^ B	Set of elements to specifically one of A or B

Example Program

A = {1,2,3,4,5}

B = {2,4,6,8}

C = A|B

D = A&B

if c> D:

  print("C is superset of D")

elif C < D:

  print("C is subset of D")

Output

C is superset of D

6.4.   Dictionaries

A Python known-data type that stores both the key and their value as asset is called the dictionaries. The dictionaries are also known as the associative array or a hash table.

Example: x = {1: "Apple", 2: "Banana", 3: "Grapes"}

The key and the value are paired together and are placed with the curly brackets to a dictionary, x.

6.4.1.   *Need of Dictionaries*

The dictionary pairs the key and the value of an element using the hash table method. Due to this internal process, accessing a value in dictionary through its key value is considered faster. Therefore, we need dictionaries for fast and optimistic operations.

6.4.2.   *Basics of Dictionaries*

The dictionaries are unordered and mutable data formats. While creating a dictionary, a key has to be given prominent importance because,

- i). Keys remain as the unique objects within the dictionaries.
- ii). Keys must belong to the immutable data types such as strings, numbers or tuples, while value can be of any of the Python data types.
- iii). Due to the immutable property, the keys remain unchangeable while the values assigned to them are subjected to any sort of modifications.
- iv). Keys are capable of holding any number of values.

6.4.3.   *Creating a Dictionary*

The dictionaries are created by placing the pair of key and value within the curly or set brackets. The elements are separated using the commas, while the key and value are facilitated with colons.

Example Program

```
x ={1:"one", 2:"two",3:"three"}
print("Dictionary x =",x)
print(type(x))
```

Output

```
Dictionary x = {1: 'one', 2: 'two', 3: 'three'}
<class 'dict'>
```

Create a dictionary using the dict ( ) function:

The built-in Python function that creates a dictionary by taking a subjective number of key-value pairs as the arguments is the dict ( ) function.

- dict (keyword arguments)

Example Program

```
marks = dict(eng = 89, math= 100, science =98, arts =90)
print("Dictionary Marks =",marks)
print(type(marks))
```

Output

```
Dictionary Marks = {'eng': 89, 'math': 100, 'science': 98, 'arts':
90}
<class 'dict'>
```

- dict (mapping, keyword arguments)

Example Program

```
s = dict({"Apple":5, "Orange": 7, "Grapes": 6}, Pineapple =9)
print ("Dictionary s =",s)
print(type(s))
```

Output

```
Dictionary s = {'Apple': 5, 'Orange': 7, 'Grapes': 6, 'Pineapple':
9}
<class 'dict'>
```

- dict (list of tuples)

Here the first argument of the tuple becomes the key and the second argument as the value of the dictionary.

Example Program

```
employees = dict([("Eno001", 15000),("Eno002",10000),
        ("Eno003",20000)])
print("Dictionary Employees =",employees)
print(type(employees))
```

Output

```
Dictionary Employees = {'Eno001': 15000, 'Eno002': 10000,
'Eno003': 20000}
<class 'dict'>
```

- dict (zip(list, list))

Example Program

```
subjects = ["Eng", "Math", "Science","Arts"]
marks = [89,100,98,97]
marksheet = dict(zip(subjects,marks))
print("Dictionary Marksheet =",marksheet)
print(type(marksheet))
```

Output

```
Dictionary Marksheet = {'Eng': 89, 'Math': 100, 'Science': 98,
'Arts': 97}
<class 'dict'>
```

Accessing Value from a Dictionary

Since dictionaries are unordered collection of items, accessing an item by using its index value as if used in the tuples and lists are not possible. So to access a value from a dictionary, the key has eo be embedded within the square brackets [ ].

Example Problem

```
x ={ 1:"one", 2:"two",3:"three"}
print("Dictionary x =",x)
print("Accessing dictionary:",x[2])
```

Output

```
Dictionary x = {1: 'one', 2: 'two', 3: 'three'}
Accessing dictionary: two
```

6.4.4.   Adding and Replacing Values

Adding Values

- **Single value:** The square brackets with key and assigned value.

Example Program

```
x ={ 1:"one", 2:"two",3:"three"}
print("Dictionary x =",x)
x[4] = "four"
print("Updated Dictionary x =",x)
```

Output

```
Dictionary x = {1: 'one', 2: 'two', 3: 'three'}
 Updated Dictionary x = {1: 'one', 2: 'two', 3: 'three', 4: 'four'}
```

- **Multiple values:** The update ( ) of method takes either a dictionary or a tuple or a list as the arguments and updates an existing dictionary.

Example Program

```
x ={1:"one", 2:"two",3:"three"}
print("Dictionary x =",x)
x.update({4:"four",5:"five"})
print("Updated Dictionary x =",x)
```

Output

```
Dictionary x = {1: 'one', 2: 'two', 3: 'three'}
Updated Dictionary x = {1: 'one', 2: 'two', 3: 'three', 4: 'four',
5: 'five'}
```

Replacing Values

- **Single value:** A value of dictionary can be replaced by using the existing key with a new value.

Example Program

```
x ={ 1:"one", 2:"two",3:"three"}
print("Dictionary x =",x)
x[3] = "number"
print("Replaced value:",x)
```

Output

```
Dictionary x = {1: 'one', 2: 'two', 3: 'three'}
Replaced value: {1: 'one', 2: 'two', 3: 'number'}
```

- **Multiple values:** The update ( ) with existing key can replace and overwrite the key values.

Example Program

```
x ={1:"one", 2:"two",3:"three"}
print("Dictionary x =",x)
x.update({1:"Odd",2:"Even", 3:"Odd"})
print("Updated Dictionary x =",x)
```

Output

```
Dictionary x = {1: 'one', 2: 'two', 3: 'three'}
Updated Dictionary x = {1: 'Odd', 2: 'Even', 3: 'Odd'}
```

6.4.5. Retrieving Values

If a dictionary has been accessed through an undefined key, an exception called the keyError has been raised.

To overcome this exception, dict.get (key [, default]) has been used and this method,

    i).   Returns the key value if exist.

    ii).   Returns the default value if exists and key does not exist.

    iii).   Returns none, if both default and key doesn't exist.

Example Program

```
x ={1:"one", 2:"two",3:"three"}
print("Dictionary x =",x)
print("Existing key 2: ",x.get(2))
print("Non-Existing key 4: ",x.get(4))
```

Output

```
Dictionary x = {1: 'one', 2: 'two', 3: 'three'}
Existing key 2:  two
Non-Existing key 4:  None
```

6.4.6. Formatting Dictionaries

The Python keyword format has been used format the dictionaries. The following program has been used the format keyword to print a given dictionary in a table format.

Example Program

```
fruits = {1: ["Apple", 5, 800],2: ["Orange", 2, 300],
   3: ["Grapes", 4, 400], }
print ("{:<10} {:<10} {:<10}".format('FRUIT', 'KG', 'PRICE'))
for key, value in fruits.items():
    fruit,kg, price = value
    print ("{:<10} {:<10} {:<10}".format(fruit, kg, price))
```

Output

```
FRUIT    KG     PRICE
Apple    5      800
Orange   2      300
Grapes   4      400
```

6.4.7. Deleting Items

The Python built-in methods that are used to delete or remove dictionary elements are:-

- **del ()**–The del function deletes the entire dictionary without any specification.

Example Program

```
X = {1: "One", 2:"Two",3:"Three"}
print("Dictionary X:",X)
del X[2]
print("New Dictionary X:",X)
```

Output

```
Dictionary X: {1: 'One', 2: 'Two', 3: 'Three'}
New Dictionary X: {1: 'One', 3: 'Three'}
```

- **pop ()** – A item that belongs to a specific key has been removed using this function.

Example Program

```
X = {1: "One", 2:"Two",3:"Three",4:"Four"}
print("Dictionary X:",X)
X.pop(3)
print("New Dictionary X:",X)
```

Output

```
Dictionary X: {1: 'One', 2: 'Two', 3: 'Three', 4: 'Four'}
New Dictionary X: {1: 'One', 2: 'Two', 4: 'Four'}
```

- **popitem()** – If no keys specified, then the function mostly removes the last item of the dictionary or any arbitrary item.

Example Program

```
X = {1: "One", 2:"Two",3:"Three",4:"Four"}
print("Dictionary X:",X)
X.popitem()
print("New Dictionary X:",X)
```

Output

```
Dictionary X: {1: 'One', 2: 'Two', 3: 'Three', 4: 'Four'}
New Dictionary X: {1: 'One', 2: 'Two', 3: 'Three'}
```

- **Clear()** – This function removes all the elements of a dictionary making it empty.

Example Program

```
X = {1: "One", 2:"Two",3:"Three",4:"Four"}

print("Dictionary X:",X)

X.clear()

print("New Dictionary X:",X)
```

Output

```
Dictionary X: {1: 'One', 2: 'Two', 3: 'Three', 4: 'Four'}

New Dictionary X: {}
```

6.4.8. Comparing Two Dictionaries

- To find duplicate keys by comparing two dictionary:- d1.keys () & d2.keys ()
- To find the difference in the keys:- d1.keys ()- d2.keys ()
- To find key-value pairs in common:- d1.items() && d2.items ( )

Example Program

```
d1 = {"Fruit":"Apple", "Kg":1,"Price":150}

d2 = {"fruit":"Orange", "kg":1,"Price":80, "Color":"Orange"}

d3 = {"fruit":"Orange", "kg":2,"Price":80, "Color":"Yellow"}

d4 = {"Friut":"Apple", "Weight":3, "Rate": 170}

print("To find the Duplicate Keys:\n")

print("Comparing d1 and d2:", d1.keys() & d2.keys())

print("Comparing d1 and d4:", d1.keys() & d4.keys())

print("Comparing d4 and d1:", d4.keys() & d1.keys())

print("\nTo find difference in the keys:\n")

print("Comparing d2 and d3:", d2.keys()- d3.keys())

print("Comparing d1 and d4:", d1.keys() - d4.keys())

print("\nTo find key:value pairs in commom:\n")

print("Comparing d2 and d3:", d2.items() - d3.items())

print("Comparing d2 and d3:", d3.items() - d2.items())
```

Output

To find the Duplicate Keys:

Comparing d1 and d2: {'Price'}
Comparing d1 and d4: set()
Comparing d4 and d1: set()

To find difference in the keys:

Comparing d2 and d3: set()
Comparing d1 and d4: {'Kg', 'Price', 'Fruit'}

To find key:value pairs in commom:

Comparing d2 and d3: {('Color', 'Orange'), ('kg', 1)}
Comparing d2 and d3: {('Color', 'Yellow'), ('kg', 2)}

6.4.9. *The Methods of Dictionary Class*

The following methods and functions are applied to dictionary class,

1	copy ()	Creates a duplicate copy of the given dictionary.
2	clear ()	Creates an empty dictionary by deleting all the elements
3	pop ()	With the key provided, the function removes and returns elements an element of the given dictionary.
4	get ()	To have the value of a particular key.
5	items ()	Returns the elements of a dictionary as a key-value pairs.
6	keys ()	The objects of all keys present in a dictionary are returned through this function.
7	popitem ()	An item has been removed and returned, mostly the last item.
8	setdefault ()	If a key doesn't exist, the function inserts a key and its value.
9	update ()	Adds and updates the key-value pair of a dictionary.
10	values ( )	The function provides all the values of a dictionary.
11	hash_key ()	If a particular key exist, the function returns TRUE else FLASE.
12	fromkeys()	With a sequence of key and values, a new dictionary has been created.

6.4.10. Traversing Dictionaries

During any operation with the key-value pairs, the traversing through the dictionaries takes place by using loops and methods like keys () method and items () method.

Example Program

```
f = {1:"Apple", 2:"Banana", 3:"Lemon"}
print("Traversing dictionary using keys():")
for k in f.keys():
  print(k,f[k])
```

Output

```
Traversing dictionary using keys():
1 Apple
2 Banana
3 Lemon
```

Example Program

```
f = {1:"Apple", 2:"Banana", 3:"Lemon"}
print("Traversing dictionary using items():")
for x,y in f.items():
  print(x,y)
```

Output

```
Traversing dictionary using items():
1 Apple
2 Banana
3 Lemon
```

By using items ( ) method, a list of tuples has been returned where each tuples hold a key and its value. While printing a dictionary item, each tuple has been unpacked to two separated variables at a time.

6.4.11. Nested Dictionaries

When a dictionary is created by using one or more dictionaries as the items, then the dictionary is known as the nested dictionary. In other words, the nested dictionary is a collection of dictionaries.

```
nd= { d1:{...... }, d2: {......},....,dn:{......}}
```

nd is the nested dictionary of d1, d2 which are placed inside thend. The d1, d2 will have their own key: value pairs.

Create a Nested Dictionary

Example Program

```
nest_d = {1 : {1:101,2:102,3:103}, 2 : {1:201,2:202,3:203},

3 : {1:301, 2:302, 3:303}}

print("Nested dictionary nest_d:")

print(nest_d)

print(type(nest_d))
```

Output

```
Nested dictionary nest_d:

{1: {1: 101, 2: 102, 3: 103}, 2: {1: 201, 2: 202, 3: 203},

 3: {1: 301, 2: 302, 3: 303}}

<class 'dict'>
```

Accessing a Nested Dictionary

To access an element of a nested dictionary, the indexing has been used. The dictionary and its key are specified by using the square brackets [ ].

Example Program

```
sub = {1:{"eng" : 89,"math" : 78, "sci" : 98},

    2:{"eng" :90,"math" : 89, "sci" :90},

    3:{"eng" : 87, "math" : 100, "sci" : 99}}

print("Math in dictionary 1:",sub[1]["math"])

print("Eng in dictionary 2:",sub[2]["eng"])

print("Math in dictionary 3:",sub[3]["sci"])
```

Output

```
Math in dictionary 1: 78

Eng in dictionary 2: 90

Math in dictionary 3: 99
```

Update a Nested Dictionary

Example Program

```
sub = {1:{"eng" : 89,"math" : 78, "sci" : 98},

    2:{"eng" :90,"math" : 89, "sci" :90},

    3:{"eng" : 87, "math" : 100, "sci" : 99}}

print("Updating a nested dictionary:")

sub[4] = {}

sub[4]["eng"] = 96

sub[4]["math"] = 91

sub[4]["sci"] = 80

sub[2]["eng"] = 88

print(sub)
```

Output

```
Updating a nested dictionary:

{1: {'eng': 89, 'math': 78, 'sci': 98},

 2: {'eng': 88, 'math': 89, 'sci': 90},

 3: {'eng': 87, 'math': 100, 'sci': 99},

 4: {'eng': 96, 'math': 91, 'sci': 80}}
```

Delete a Nested Dictionary

Example Program

```
sub = {1: {'eng': 89, 'math': 78, 'sci': 98},

    2: {'eng': 88, 'math': 89, 'sci': 90},

    3: {'eng': 87, 'math': 100, 'sci': 99},

    4: {'eng': 96, 'math': 91, 'sci': 80}}

print("Deleting a key:")

del sub[3]["math"]

print (sub)

print("Deleting a dictionary:")

del sub[4]

print(sub)
```

Deleting a key:

{1: {'eng': 89, 'math': 78, 'sci': 98},

 2: {'eng': 88, 'math': 89, 'sci': 90},

3: {'eng': 87, 'sci': 99},

4: {'eng': 96, 'math': 91, 'sci': 80}}

Deleting a dictionary:

{1: {'eng': 89, 'math': 78, 'sci': 98},

2: {'eng': 88, 'math': 89, 'sci': 90},

 3: {'eng': 87, 'sci': 99}}

6.4.12. Traversing Nested Dictionaries

Example Program

```
g = {1:{"Name":"Alex", "Place":"America","Animal":"Anaconda",
"Thing":"Alarm"},
   2:{"Name":"Python","Place":"Paris","Animal":"Python",
"Thing":"Pen"}}
for x, y in g.items():
 print("\nGame:",x)
 for key in y:
    print(key + ':', y[key])
```

Output

Game: 1

Name: Alex

Place: America

Animal: Anaconda

Thing: Alarm

Game: 2

Name: Python

Place: Paris

Animal: Python

Thing: Pen

6.4.13. Simple Programs on Dictionaries

Example Program

Program to print a dictionary in both Ascending and Descending Orders

```python
import operator
d = {1: "A", 2:"D", 3: "B", 4:"F" , 5:"C", 6:"E"}
print("Given dictionary : ",d)
a_sort = sorted(d.items(), key=operator.itemgetter(1))
print("Ascending order: ",a_sort)
d_sort = dict( sorted(d.items(), key=
operator.itemgetter(1),reverse=True))
print("Descending order:",d_sort)
```

Output

```
Given dictionary:  {1: 'A', 2: 'D', 3: 'B', 4: 'F', 5: 'C', 6: 'E'}
Ascending order:  [(1, 'A'), (3, 'B'), (5, 'C'), (2, 'D'),
(6, 'E'), (4, 'F')]
Descending order: {4: 'F', 6: 'E', 2: 'D', 5: 'C', 3: 'B', 1: 'A'}
```

Example Program

Program to print same key: value pairs in given two dictionaries

```python
v = {1:"a", 2:"u",3:"i",4:"o",5:"e"}
a = {1:"a",2:"b",3:"c",4:"d",5:"e"}
print("Same keys in two dictionaries in v and a:")
for (key, value) in set(v.items()) & set(a.items()):
    print('%s: %s ' % (key, value))
```

Output

```
Same keys in two dictionaries in v and a:
1: a
5: e
```

6.4.14. Polynomials of Dictionaries

The immutable data types of python are integers, float-value, strings, complex number and tuples while the lists and dictionaries are mutable. The content of the dictionary are mutable but the keys present in the dictionary are immutable types. Therefore, the keys in a dictionary may be of any of the above mentioned Python immutable data types and not be of lists because lists are mutable. Mostly commonly the integers are used as the keys in dictionaries.

A polynomialcan be considered as dictionary, by accounting the powers and coefficient as the key: value pairs.

$$P(x) = -1 + x^2 + 3x^7$$

From the above polynomial p, the integers play the role as the keys in the dictionary. By considering the above polynomial, the set of powers and coefficient pairs are used to map them into a dictionary as p = {0:-1,2: 1, 7:3}

Summary

This Chapter covers the data types in Python which includes list, tuple, set and dictionary. The built-in functions and methods associated with list, tuple, set and dictionary is illustrated with examples.

References

[1]   www. tutorialspoint.com

[2]   www.educba.com

[3]   www.iteanz.com

[4]   www.pythoncentral.io

[5]   www.codedestine.com

[6]   www.railsware.com

[7]   www.dyclassroom.com

[8]   www.programiz.com

[9]   www.w3schools.com

[10]   www.docs.python.org

[11]   www.thispointer.com

[12]   www.towardsdatascience.com

[13]   www.hplgit.github.io

6.5.   Test Your Skill

Multiple Choice Questions

1. The ____________ are created using any number of variables of different data types such as integer, float and string.

    a) Tuples

    b) Lists

    c) Sets

    d) None of the mentioned

2. The tuples without parentheses are known as ____________
   a) Tuple variable
   b) Tuple Packing
   c) Tuple set
   d) Dictionaries

3. To convert a given list into a tuple, ____________ has been used.
   a) tuple(list)
   b) tuple(sequence)
   c) tuple (seq)
   d) tuple(sq)

4. To access a particular part of the tuple, the ____________ has been used.
   a) Slice-in operator
   b) Access operator
   c) Slicing operator
   d) None of the mentioned

5. To find out whether a given element is present within a tuple, the ____________ operator has been used.
   a) In
   b) Out
   c) Into
   d) Onto

6. Python aids us to create a function that is capable of processing multiple numbers of arguments known as ____________
   a) Function with same arguments
   b) Function with variable length arguments
   c) Function with fixed length arguments
   d) None of the mentioned

7. A sequential collection of data within the square brackets [ ] are called ____________
   a) Dictionaries
   b) Sets
   c) Tuples
   d) Lists

8. A ______________ is a collection of elements that are unordered, immutable and has the hash table, a data structure as the foundation.

   a) Python set

   b) Python list

   c) Python tuple

   d) Python dictionary

9. A Python known-data type that stores both the key and their value as asset is called the

   ____

   a) Tuples

   b) Dictionaries

   c) Lists

   d) Sets

10. When a dictionary is created by using one or more dictionaries as the items, then the dictionary is known as the ______________

   a) Dictionary collection

   b) Dictionary set

   c) Nested dictionary

   d) Multi-dictionary

Review Questions

1. What are lists and tuples in Python?

2. What are sets in Python?

3. How do you create dictionary in Python?

4. What is the difference between tuples and lists in Python?

5. How do you get all the values in dictionary?

7. Exception Handling

Learning Outcomes

- Introduction on Exception handling in Python.
- Types of Exception handling.
- Detailed Illustration on Exception Handling functions.
- Illustration on User-defined function.
- Various Applications of exception handling.

Introduction

Errors are the mistakes or the analytical breakdown in a program that have been interfered by the Python Interpreter during the process of execution. Syntax errors and Exceptions are the major types of errors considered in Python Programming. The Syntactic errors are the ridiculous errors caused by the programmers by presenting the wrong syntax. But the Exceptions are raised, even with the perfect syntax and systematical structure of program due to an unexpected cause that leads to the weirdness in the programming execution.

One of the popular examples to explain Exception is ZeroDivisionError. Consider the following arithmetic program; the Python executes very single line without any interruption until it reaches the last line. There comes the exception stating the ZeroDivisionError, which is division by zero is not accepted by the Python Interpreter. Thus, an Exception has been raised.

```
a = 5
b = 0
print ("Addition: a + b =", a+b)
print ("Subtraction: a – b = ", a-b)
print ("Multiplication: a*b = ", a*b)
print ("Division: a/b = ", a/b)
```

Some of the other examples that explains the Exception are:

- An exception has been raised when we try to open a file that does not exist.
- An exception has been raised when an uncongenial data types has been provided instead of the requested ones.
- An exception has been raised when we try to access a database that has been disconnected from the server.

7.1. What is Exception Handling?

Exceptions are raised during the execution and only when the result of the given code shows an error, while the program has the accurate lexical and syntax. The program won't be terminated due to the raise of an exception, yet it produces a difference in the natural flow of the program and the operations that have been carried so far would be lost.

When the logical and reasoning about a particular block of coding lacks, the Python Interpreter stops the execution process and try to find a suitable solution to overcome the situation, significant measures are taken. That has been defines as the Exception Handling.

Help (Execution) – the code on the Python script afford to acknowledge us the intact comprehension about the Exception class.

Like functions, the Exception handling in Python is for the two types of exceptions:

- In - built Exceptions
- User - defined Exceptions

The following table represents the in-built Python Exceptions:

	Exceptions	Raised
1	ArithmeticError	If any numeric operational errors occur and also a base class.
2	AssertionError	If the Assert statement does not succeed.
3	AttributeError	If the reference or an assignment goes not succeed.
4	EnvironmentError	Fundamental class for each and every exception that occurs external to the Python environment.
5	EoFError	If the interpreter reaches the end of the file without receiving any input from the input () function.
6	FloatingPointError	If a floating point operation does not successfully return the result.
7	ImportError	If the import statement does not succeed.
8	IndentationError	If there exist error in the indentation.
9	IndexError	If a particular sequence does not have any index.
10	IOError	If the Input/Output operations like the print () or open () statements does not succeed.
11	KeyboardInterrupt	If the programmer interrupts the execution, generally with Ctrl + C.
12	KeyError	If a dictionary does not hold any particular key.
13	NameError	If an identifier is missing in either the local or the global namespace.
14	NotImplementedError	If the abstract to a particular inherited class has been failed to be properly implemented.
15	OverflowError	If a particular operation goes beyond a fixed limit of a specific type of the number system.
16	RuntimeError	If an error apart from the mentioned exception types.
17	StandardError	Fundamental class for every in-built exception, apart from StopIteration and SystemExit.
18	StopIteration	If for an iterator, the next () method does not imply to any particular object.
19	SyntaxError	If a particular Python syntax has been written wrong.
20	SystemError	If an error occurs within the Python Interperter.
21	SystemExit	If the sys.exit () function is used to terminate the Python Interpreter.
22	TypeError	If the calculation are done with data types that does not match with the mentioned ones.
23	UnboundLocalError	If a local variable with no assignment has been called by a function or a method.
24	ValueError	If an in-built function has a valid types of arguments but the arguments doesn't hold the right values.
25	ZeroDivisionError	If the division has been calculated with the divider as zero, irrespective of the data type.

7.2.   How Exception Handling is Used in Python?

The Exceptions are used to be the class objects that are prompted spontaneously, if the Python Interpreter identifies any error. The following five statements as the Exception Handlers to be the class objects are used in Python,

- *Try/except*

The statement has been a bond of try clause and the except clause. The try clause hold the programming coding that are likely expected to raise the exceptions while the except clause contains the counter code that handles the exception that is the class objects and arguments.

Syntax

```
try:
        operations
        ..........
except:
        if there is exception
        ..........
else:
        if no exception
        ..........
```

- *Try/Finally*

The finally statement as the final statement to try statement and has been executed no matter what the try clause holds. It works as the closing statement as a concluding argument or an expression or an action such as closing of a file, disconnecting the server or the database.

Syntax

```
try:
        operations
        ..........
except:
        if there is exception
        ..........
else:
        if no exception
        ..........
finally:
        unconditional execution
        ....
```

- ***Assert***

If any two variables are suppose to be compared, they are subject as the conditional arguments to the Assert statement which returns a Boolean value of either TRUE or FALSE as the result. If the result is true, the consecutive line has been executed else the Python Interpreter terminated the program execution.

Syntax

assert< condition>

- ***Raise***

The Raise statement has been used to determine the interpretation of the Python language of handling the exceptions. The statement clearly specifies the declaration of the exceptions and triggers the code for the particular exception.

Syntax

raise[Exception [, args[, traceback]]]
args – Arguments holds the values for the exceptions if any exists.
Traceback – An optional argument.

7.3. Except Clause

A common except clause has the ability to handle any sort of exceptions. The exceptions mentioned within the Except block has been executed only if the Try block contains that specific exception- circumstance. Since the Except block has been executed with such an if-condition, the else part has been included as the Else block. The Except block experience is based on any of the following situations:

Case 1: Except clause with No Exception – If there is no exception raised, the except clause works as an optional code and the else clause will be executed.

Case 2: Except clause with Multiple Exceptions – If a particular operation has been suspect to produce different types of exceptions, a single Try clause and Except clause can have multiple exception statements.

Syntax

try:

operations

....

        except(exception1[, exception 2[, ...exception n[ ]]]):

                if there is exceptions

                ....

        else:

                ifno exceptions

                ....

Example Program 1

        n = 20

        try:

                d = n/0

                 print(d)

        except ZeroDivisionError:

                print("Error: Division by Zero not allowed!!!")

Output

                Error: Division by Zero not allowed!!!

Example Program 2

        try:

          a= open ("apple","r")

          a. write("fruit")

        except IOError:

          print("Error: can't find the file")

        else:

            print("Apple is a fruit")

Output

        Error: can't find the file

Disadvantages of Try- Except

The Try-Except statements are not mostly recommend because of their ability to catch all sort of exceptions significantly, but they lack to recognize the source of the problem that may happen.

7.4.   Try and Finally Clause

The finally has been execute after the normal termination of try block or after block terminates due to some execution.

Try Statement

Try statement is one of the exception handling mechanism that includes the keyword "try" continued by a colon (:) and a block of program coding which are expected to raise an exception. By executing the program either of the following causes might raise:

Case 1: No Exception – The Python Interpreter disregards the exception handlers for that specific try statement.

Case 2: Exception Exist – The program control moves on to the pairing exceptions.

Finally Statement

The Finally clause is an optional block that has been defined to concentrated effort on the actions which has been executed in any sort of arising conditions. The block has been executed regardless of whether there exists an exception or not. The statement begins with the "finally" keyword and a colon (:) following the try statement.

Syntax

```
Try:

        Operations

        ............

Except:

        If there is Exception

        .........

Else:

        No exception

        .........

Finally

        Executed unconditionally

        .........
```

7.5.   Programs on Try and Finally Clause

Program 1: Program for ZeroDivisionError Exception using Try...Finally

Coding:

```
try:

        a = int(input("Enter a number lesser than 5: "))
        b = int(input("Enter a number greater than 5: "))
        c = b/a
```

```python
except ZeroDivisionError:
 print(" 'a' value not be zero")
else:
 print("Division: ", c)
finally:
  print("This is a simple program")
```

Output 1:

Enter a number lesser than 5: 4

Enter a number greater than 5: 8

Division: 2.0

This is a simple program

Output 2:

Enter a number lesser than 5: 0

Enter a number greater than 5: 6

'a' value not be zero

This is a simple program

Program 2: Program with any two in-built Exceptions

Coding:

```python
try:
 a = {1:"Apple", 2:"Banana", 3:"Cirtus", 4:"Dargon Fruit"}
 b = {1:"A", 2:"B", 3:"C"}
 n = int(input("Enter your choice ( 0/1): "))
 if (n == 0):
   assert a == b
 else:
   print(a[5])
   raise LookupError
except AssertionError:
 print("Comparison done")
except LookupError:
 print(" The dictionary a{} does not have a[5]")
finally:
 print("This is a Built-in Exception")
```

Enter your choice (0/1): 0

Comparison done

This is a Built-in Exception

Output 2

Enter your choice (0/1): 1

The dictionary a{} does not have a[5]

This is a Built-in Exception

7.6.   User Defined Exceptions

Python allows the programmers to create their own exceptions based on their suspensions and expectations. The built-in exceptions are still used as the base class to create the user-defined exceptions, either directly or indirectly. To differentiate and identify the user designed exception from the standard exceptions, the user–made exception classes are terminated with the term "Error".

- ***User-defined Multiple Exceptions***

To define a module with a number of individual exceptions, a strong base class has been classified with several subclasses for the individual exceptions.

Example Program

```
class Error(Exception):
  # Base class for other Exceptions
  pass
class DividebyZero (Error):
  # Raised when the input is zero
  pass
try:
        n = int(input ("Enter a number:"))
        if n == 0:
                raise DividebyZero
except DividebyZero:
        print("Oops! Not zero")
else:
        print("Division :", n/2)
```

Output 1

Enter a number:0

Oops! Not zero

Output 2

Enter a number:8

Division: 4.0

- ### User-defined Standard Exceptions

If suppose an error elevates but does not belong to any of above discussed kind of exceptions, an in-built class called the Runtime Error has been called.

Example Program

```
class Usererror(RuntimeError):
        def __init__(self, value):
                self.args = value
try:
        raise Usererror("userError")
except Usererror as e:
        print (e.args)
```

Output

('u', 's', 'e', 'r', 'E', 'r', 'r', 'o', 'r')

7.7.   Programs on User Defined Exceptions

Program 1: Finding the Grades according the given mark using User Defined Exceptions

```
Program coding:-
class grade_Error(Exception):
 n = str(input ("Name:"))
 pass
class O_grade(Error):
 pass
class A_grade(Error):
 pass
class B_grade(Error):
```

```python
 pass
class C_grade(Error):
 pass
class Fail(Error):
 pass
try:
  m = int(input("Enter the mark: "))
  if m == 100:
    print("Excellect")
  elif m >= 90:
   raise A_grade
  elif m >= 75:
    raise B_grade
  elif m >= 50:
    raise C_grade
  else:
    raise Fail
except A_grade:
 print("A")
except B_grade:
 print("B")
except C_grade:
 print("C")
except Fail:
 print("Oops!!! Better Luck next time")
finally:
  print("Your Grade in paper: Python")
  Output 1:
Name:Priya
Enter the mark: 56
C
Your Grade in paper: Python
Output 2:
Name:Aarav
```

Enter the mark: 32

Oops!!! Better Luck next time

Your Grade in paper: Python

Output 3:

Name:Vijay

Enter the mark: 100

Excellect

Your Grade in paper: Python

Program 2: Check Voter's Eligibility using User Defined Exceptions

Program Coding:

```
class VoterError (Exception):
 input("Enter your name: ")
 pass
class not_adult(Error):
 pass
try:
 a = int(input("Age: "))
 if a <=17 :
  raise not_adult
except not_adult:
 print("Sorry!!, Not Eligible")
else:
 print("Hooray!, You are Eligible!!!!")
 Output 1:
Enter your name: John
Age: 18
Hooray!,You are Eligible!!!!
Output 2:
Enter your name: Chanak
Age: 5
Sorry!!, Not Eligible
```

Program 3: *Program to have both User Defined and Built-in Exceptions*

Program Coding:

```
class myprogram(Exception):
 pass
class builtin(NameError):
 pass
class singleError(Error):
 pass
class positive(Error):
 pass
try:
 print("User Defined Exception:\n")
 n = int (input("Enter any number:"))
 if (n<=9):
   raise singleError
except singleError:
 a = print("Given Number is a SINGLE Digit Number")
else:
 print("Given Number is a DOUBLE Digit Number")
try:
 print("\nBuilt-in Exception:\n")
 print(Num)
 raise NameError
except NameError:
 print("'Num' does not exist")
finally:
   print("Both Exceptions are executed successfully!!!")
```

Output 1:

User Defined Exception:

Enter any number:6

Given Number is a SINGLE Digit Number

Built-in Exception:

'Num' does not exist

Both Exceptions are executed successfully!!!

Output 2:

User Defined Exception:

Enter any number:45

Given Number is a DOUBLE Digit Number

Built-in Exception:

'Num' does not exist

Both Exceptions are executed successfully!!!

7.8. Applications of Exception Handling

1. Error Handling:

The exceptions are used to spot out the errors during the execution time of a program and produce a drastic change in the program behavior. The 'try – except' as the Exception Handler are used by the programmers to handle the exception in versatile manner.

2. Signal Notification:

The exceptions are used to notify the appropriate circumstance and their solutions, by conveying them conservatively.

3. Execution Extinction:

To exit some of the critical or need-to –be-fixed errors, the execution are the best in handling the exceptions. The best example to support this point is the 'try- finally' statements, an end/ close of the problem has been proposed in the finally statement explicitly.

4. Dramatic Flow of the Control:

The programmers can also use the exceptions as a basic for implementing unusual control flow. Since there is no 'go-to' statement in Python, the exceptions can be a help with this perceptive.

5. Prevents Potential Failures:

The Exception Handling works as a Python object that correspond to the errors by highlighting them and enforcing   the programmers to rectify those problematic conditions.

Thus, Exception Handling has been an aid to secure the programs from being stopped or crashed out in a hysterical way.

7.9. Advantages and Disadvantages of Exception Handling

Advantages

1. The exceptions exclusively include both the proved and the unproved type of errors but significantly consider the unproven ones and make the Python programming environment stronger to overcome the challenging circumstances.
2. If an unexpected error occurs and the program is in need of the recovery, the exceptions handle the situation with higher precept and prominent recovery.
3. The Exceptions separate the problematic and the susceptive codes from the original logical programming stream. This differentiating property of clearing out the normal codes and the Error handling codes provides an advantage to the programmers.
4. The error reporting and solving it with a call function is also an advantage. The exceptions are capable of reporting and handling the error by rising and call a particular solvent.
5. Categorizing and classifying of the types of errors based on the hierarchy of the classes, the exceptions as the objects are grouped and organized.

Disadvantages

1. The immense drawback of an exception is that they are raised during the time of execution and leads to distraction of the program causing the entire lose of logical operations calculated so far.
2. Some of the exceptions are totally unexpected, since they occurs external to the Python program such as IO device disorders.
3. If an exception happens inexpertly and causes the execution of the program to stop, it may leads to serious damages to the resources that are connected to the program namely the files, database and the other IO sources.
4. Another inconvenience of the exception handling, the raise of an exception might make the process the slow and eventually the program size increase because of the add-on cautioner codes.

Summary

This chapter covers exception handling mechanisms, built-in exception, handling exceptions using try.... except, except clause, try... finally statements. It also covers, how to raise an exception, user-defined exception and assertions in Python.

References

[1]   www.geeksforgeeks.com

[2]   www.tutorialspoint.com

[3]   www.w3schools.com

[4]   www.guru99.com

[5]   www.netjstech.com

7.10. Test Your Skill

Multiple Choice Question

1. Errors are the mistakes or the analytical breakdown in a program that have been interfered by the Python ____________ during the process of execution.

    1) Interpreter

    2) Complier

    3) Assembler

    4) None of the mentioned

2. ____________ are raised during the execution only when the result of the given code shows an error, while the program has the accurate lexical and syntax.

    a) Logical flaws

    b) Exceptions

    c) Mistakes

    d) None of the mentioned

3. Which of the following is not an in-built python exception?

    a) EOFError

    b) IOError

    c) EFError

    d) KeyError

4. Which error is raised when a local variable with no assignment has been called by a function or a method?

    a) UnboundLocalError

    b) BoundLocalError

    c) LocalError

    d) GlobalError

5. The _____________ clause hold the programming coding that are likely expected to raise the exceptions while the _____________ clause contains the counter code that handles the exception that is the class objects and arguments.

    a) Try, finally
    b) Finally, try
    c) Try, except
    d) Except, try

6. The _____________ statement as the final statement to try statement and has been executed no matter what the _____________ clause holds.

    a) Try, finally
    b) Finally, try
    c) Try, except
    d) Except, try

7. The _____________ statement has been used to determine the interpretation of the Python language of handling the exceptions.

    a) Assert
    b) Try
    c) Finally
    d) Raise

8. The exceptions mentioned within the _____________ block have been executed only if the Try block contains that specific exception- circumstance.

    a) Try
    b) Except
    c) Finally
    d) Final

9. Try statement is one of the exception handling mechanism that includes the keyword "try" continued by a _____________

    a) :
    b) ;
    c) –
    d) !

10. The ______________ clause is an optional block that has been defined to concentrated effort on the actions which has been executed in any sort of arising conditions.

   a) Final

   b) Try

   c) Finally

   d) Assert

Review Questions

1. Explain Exception Handling in Python.

2. List the built-in exceptions.

3. What is try...finally in Python?

4. How to raise an exception in Python using the raise statement?

5. Write short notes on user-defined exceptions.

8. File Handling

Learning Outcomes

- Importance of File handling.
- Text and binary files in Python.
- Various operations on the text files illustrate.
- About the Seek () function.
- Details on Binary files.

8.1. Introduction

A Record is an object on the virtual platform that has data, information or commands stored for the future references. The records of a particular zone or discipline put together, collectively known as the Files. A user can create, store, view, manage and organize their precious data in the format of files deliberately known as the File Management System.

In Python, the files has been stored and viewed by using the filename with ".py" as the Python File Extension. The Python programs and their outcomes are stored in this format and are persevered for later usage. These saved files may be subject to the processes of File Handling.

Simply, File Handling is the prospect of writing and reading, to and from respectively in the stored files and is a mechanism by which various operations are executed on the saved Python instructions.

Example

To save a file in Python in the name of fruits, fruits.py has been used.

File Handling allows a Python programmer to save the outputs of the program separately and can perform numerous operations on them. The entire mechanism of File Handling has been majorly subjected within the following four processes:-

- Opening a File
- Writing to a File
- Reading from a File
- Closing a File

In Python, the file manipulation has been done as the default process with the basic operations and in-built functions.

8.2.   Need of File Handling

- **Volatile Values**: As we know in all programming languages like Python, the values of variables assigned are "volatile" in character. The values used during the run-time of a program are stored in the primary memory only and are lost. To store the value permanently and to be referred in the future, the file handling processes are used by Python in the format of files.

- **Program Outputs:** The program outputs are also stored in the files for future manipulations.

- **Processed Inputs:** There may be programs where the processed data or data derived from the external sources to be used. At such times, the files are used to store the input data making the program optimistic by reducing cost and time.

8.3.   Text Input and Output

There are two types of files accounted in Python file handling mechanism.

- Text files – filename.txt
- Binary files – filename.bin

The text files are the sequence of characters as the lines of codes which ends with a specific character termed as the "End of Line" (EOL) character. The EOL character indicated the Python Interpreter about the beginning of a new line.

8.3.1. Opening a File

To perform the file handling functions such as writing or reading the files, a file has to be opened first. Any of the following two ways can be used to open a Python file,

- To open a saved file, a Python built-in function called the open ( ) function has been used. This function with no parameters just opens the file that has been mentioned within the curly braces.

  Syntax: open (filename.txt)

Program no 1

```
opening a file named 'python1.txt'
f = open("python1.txt")
print(f.read())
```

        APPLE

        BALL

        CAT

        DOG

        EGG

- The open () function passed with the filename and the mode as the arguments. The "mode" argument indicates the functions of either read or write commonly. But Python allows the user to open the files with the following mode,

  - r, read only

  - w, write only

  - a, append only

  - r+, read and also write

Syntax: file object = open (file name, "Mode")

Program no 2

Opening a file to write only

```
x = open("python_1.txt",'w')
x.write("Hi! Welcome\n")
x.write("This is about File Handling\n ")
a = "Python Programming\n"
x.write(a)
```

Output

19

Program no 3

Opening a file to write and read

```
x = open("python_1.txt",'r+')
print(x.read())
x.write(("Interesting, isn't!"))
print(x.read())
```

Output

Hi! Welcome

This is about File Handling

Python Programming

Interesting, isn't!

The "mode" argument which is not obligatory to pass while using the open ( ) function, but the Python Interpreter assume 'r' as default.

8.3.2. Writing Text to a File

The text to be entered into a saved file, has been passed through by using the write ( ) function.

> Syntax: file object. write (" ")

Program no 4

```
f =(open("new.txt",'r+'))
print(f.read())
f.write("Python Programming")
```

Output

```
Python Programming
18
```

8.3.3. Closing a File

After that the manipulations and operations on the files are successfully executed, the files have to be saved and closed properly. The Python in-built function called the close ( ) function has been used here.

Syntax: file object. close ( )

In Python, the files get automatically closed when the Python Interpreter detects that a reference object used in the current file has been reassigned to another file. But it would be preferable for the Python programmers to use the in-built method to close the files properly.

Program no 5

```
Closing the Python file
f = open("python_1.txt",'w')
f.write("Bye!! Bye!!")
f.close()
```

8.3.4. Writing Numbers to a File

The following program is an illustration of writing number to a Python file using the write () method.

Program no 6

```
num = range(1,11)
f = open("num.txt","w")
for x in num:
    f.write(str(x))
f.close()
print("Reopening the file to view the content:\n")
f= open("num.txt",'r')
print(f.read())
```

Output

```
Reopening the file to view the content:
12345678910
```

8.3.5. Reading Text from a File

- The read ( ) method has been used to read the text data in the form of bytes from the saved text files.

Program no 7

```
a = open("poem.txt", "r")
print(a.read())
```

Output

```
Twinkle, twinkle, little star
How I wonder what you are
Up above the world so high
Like a diamond in the sky
```

- To have a specific number of characters to read and print from the saved file, the index value has to be specified within the read ( ) function.

  Syntax: variable name = file object. read (index value)

Program no 8

```
a = open("poem.txt", "r")
print(a.read(25))
```

Output

```
Twinkle, twinkle, little
```

- To read a line of text and return the data in the string format, the readline ( ) function has been used.

  Syntax: file object. readline( )

Program no 9

```
a = open("poem.txt", "r")
print(a.readline())
```

Output

Twinkle, twinkle, little star

- The readline() function reads and returns only a single line but to have multiple number of lines read and returned in the string format, the readlines() has been used.

  Syntax: file object.readlines()

Program no 10

```
a = open("poem.txt", "r")
print(a.readlines())
```

Output

['Twinkle, twinkle, little star\n', 'How I wonder what you are\n', 'Up above the world so high\n', 'Like a diamond in the sky']

8.3.6. Reading Numbers from a File

A text file saved as num.txt contains numbers 1,2,3,4 and 5 as the content. This file has been used in the following program to find the arithmetic sum of the sequence. This program reads the numbers from the saved filed and manipulates them and returns the result.

Program no 11

```
a = open("num.txt",'r')
b = a.readlines()
x =0
for n in b:
    for y in n:
        if y.isdigit() == True:
            x += int(y)
print("Addition of the sequence (1 to 5): ",x)
```

Output

Addition of the sequence (1 to 5): 15

8.3.7. Reading Multiple Items on One Line

The readlines() built-in function reads every line of the given file and returns them in a single line in the form of a list. The following program considers a text file with "one = 1, two =2, three = 3" as the content and saved as "num.txt".

Program no 12

```
x = open("num.txt", "r")
print(x.readlines())
```

Output

```
['one = 1\n', 'two = 2\n', 'three = 3\n']
```

8.3.8. Appending Data

Appending is a mode similar to the writing mode in Python. The Appending operation simply attaches the information or data at the end of the file instead of over-writing them. The Append ( ) method is much similar to that of the write ( ) method.

Program no 13

```
fruits = ["apple\n", "banana\n", "citrus\n","dargon fruit\n", "egg fruit"]
x = open("fruits.txt", 'a+')
x.writelines(fruits)
for n in x:
 print(n)
```

Output

```
apple
banana
citrus
dargon fruit
egg fruit
```

Difference between write ( ) and append ( )

The output of this program, precisely shows the difference between the write ( ) and the Append ( ) functions. Here the Append ( ) method has not restored the existing data, meanwhile it simply adds the data to the file as the last statement, but the write ( ) method will change or replace the existing data.

8.4.   The Seek ( ) Function

To change the position of the file that has be accounted in an operation, the Seek ( ) function has been used in the Python. The Seek ( ) function defines a file handle which specifies the position where the data has to be read or written in the existing file. To known the contemporary position of the value in the file, the tell() in-built has been used.

Syntax: - f.seek (n, p_r) fruits

    f = the file pointer

    n = number of positions to move forward

    p_r = point of reference

This function has no return value. The point of reference can be of any of the following argument values:-

- '0' – A default value. To place the point of reference at the beginning of the file, "0" has been used.
- '1' – To place at the current position in the file, the value has been set as "1".
- '2' – End of the file.

Program no 14

```
a = open("poem.txt","r")
a.seek(0)
print("Line no:")
print(a.tell())
print ("Line:")
print(a.readline()
a.close()
```

Output

```
Line no:
0
Line:
Twinkle, twinkle, little star
```

8.5.   Binary Files

As we know a binary byte is made up of 8 bits of 0's or 1's. A Python binary file stores the strings of binary bytes. Like Python text files, the open ( ) function has been used to open the binary file, in which the character 'b' has been passed as the mode parameter.

8.5.1 Reading Binary Files

Similar to the text files, the Python Binary files also used the read ( ) method to read the binary data from a file.

Syntax: file object = open("filename.bin", "rb")

Program no 15

```
a = open("python.bin", "rb")
print(a.read())
```

Output

```
b 'This is about Binary Files'
```

Summary

In this Chapter, you have learned the concepts of file handling which covers how to open a file, different modes of opening file, how to close a file, how to read and write data to files, various in-built methods available in file handling. This chapter also covers, reading number, text from files and binary files in Python.

References

[1]   techopedia.com

[2]   upgrad.com

[3]   softwaretestinghelp.com

[4]   geeksforgeeks.com

[5]   edureka.com

8.6.   Test Your Skills

Multiple Choice Questions

1.   What is the use of "a" in file handling?
    a)   Read
    b)   Write
    c)   Append
    d)   None of the mentioned

2. Which function is used to write all the characters?

   a) write()

   b) writecharacters()

   c) writeall()

   d) writechar()

3. Which function is used to close a file in python?

   a) Close()

   b) Stop()

   c) End()

   d) Closefile()

4. Which of the following are the modes of both writing and reading in binary format in file?

   a) wb+

   b) w

   c) wb

   d) w+

5. Which one of the following is not attributes of file?

   a) closed

   b) softspace

   c) rename

   d) mode

6. What is the current syntax of rename() a file?

   a) rename(current_file_name, new_file_name)

   b) rename(new_file_name, current_file_name,)

   c) rename(()(current_file_name, new_file_name))

   d) none of the mentioned

7. What is the use of seek() method in files?

   a) sets the file's current position at the offset

   b) sets the file's previous position at the offset

   c) sets the file's current position within the file

   d) none of the mentioned

8. Which is/are the basic I/O connections in file?

   a) Standard Input

   b) Standard Output

   c) Standard Errors

   d) All of the mentioned

9. Which of the following mode will refer to binary data?

   a) r

   b) w

   c) +

   d) b

10. In file handling, what does this terms means "r, a"?

   a) read, append

   b) append, read

   c) write, append

   d) none of the mentioned

Review Questions

1. Explain the various modes for opening a file.

2. How will you rename a file in Python?

3. Explain the seek() and tell() method in Python.

4. Explain readline, readlines and writelines method in Python.

5. How do you read binary data from a file?

www.ingramcontent.com/pod-product-compliance
Lightning Source LLC
Chambersburg PA
CBHW051825150726
47998CB00001B/294